No Ordinary Joe:
The Mentorship Principles of Barnabas

Dwayne Buhler

LUKEFIVETEN
PUBLISHING
Kitchener, ON, Canada

Dwayne K. Buhler

Scripture taken from THE HOLY BIBLE, NEW INTERNATIONAL VER-
SION. Copyright © 1973, 1978, 1984 by International Bible Society. Used by
permission of Zondervan Bible Publishers.

Printed by LukeFiveTen Publishers

Kitchener, ON, Canada

www.lukefiveten.com

ISBN:1542385202
ISBN-13:978-1542385206

DEDICATION

This book is dedicated to my father, George Buhler, who saw beyond an ugly old root, and saw a piece of art; to my Youth Pastor and mentor, Tim Tjosvold, who was willing to spend time swinging a hammer with a less-than-cooperative teenager; and to my wife, Rhonda, who allowed me to use our dining room table as a work station, encouraged me in the process, and believed that all those scattered sheets of paper could end up one day in a book. I thank God for you all. To Him be the honor and glory.

CONTENTS

No Ordinary Joe is well written, engaging, and helpful. I love the idea of a book on Barnabas-like leadership. It is much needed in this age obsessed with Davidic/Mosaic/Pauline-style leadership."

Mark Buchanan, author of *The Rest of God*

I had the joy of knowing Dwayne Buhler in Vancouver, BC, where he was the Director of Missions Fest. This book was something that I personally experienced as he embodied the leadership style found in the pages. Thanks Dwayne, for your leadership, which is truly needed in our day!

Mika Kostamo, Lead Pastor
Salem Church, Thunder Bay, ON

Dwayne Buhler explains the whys and how-tos of mentoring in a biblically-based and practical way. As a result, *No Ordinary Joe* offers valuable insights for anyone engaged in mentoring or wishing to encourage others in that direction.

Grace Fox, author of *Moving From Fear to Freedom*

FOREWARD

The life of Barnabas has always intrigued me. Here is a biblical personality who slips onto the stage of the book of Acts without great fanfare, and steps away almost without being noticed. A superficial look would say that he was an "ordinary Joe" whose story happened to be intertwined in the lives of the leadership of the early Church. However, upon further study, one sees that his influence and character make him one of the great unsung heroes of the New Testament. Far from being an "ordinary Joe," Barnabas is a person of tremendous impact.

Dwayne Buhler

INTRODUCTION:
THE DRIFTWOOD PRINCIPLE

A resignation letter sat on my desk: signed, sealed, but not delivered. As I pondered the life-changing implications and content of the single sheet of paper, my mind wandered to a long ago day on an isolated, northwestern Pacific beach. I contemplated a lesson I had learned that day, many years before, and asked myself if the step I planned on taking was the right thing to do. Should I throw in the towel? Was giving up my only option?

I tend to learn life's valuable lessons in odd places. My "classroom settings" have included a dark cavern, a deep mudhole, the underside of a broken-down car, and a grassy field next to a knocked-over beehive. I've gleaned great truths from a walk through the woods, watching my children play, or spending an afternoon on a deserted beach searching for the perfect piece of driftwood.

The teachable moment that now flooded my mind had taken place on a cool, fall afternoon when I was a child. A deserted Pacific beach served as my classroom, and my father was my teacher. A rugged piece of driftwood, rejected by nature itself, was the object of an important lesson which serves me to this day.

My father made clocks and crafts from pieces of driftwood that washed up on the stony shores near our home. It was a sunny, yet chilly fall afternoon when he invited me to go with him to spend some time together as beachcombers.

I was eager to help my dad so when we got to the beach I literally ran from one pile of driftwood to another. I thought I was being helpful by dragging out large roots that seemed perfect. Unfortunately, he was looking for something specific, and the truth is that I only got in the way.

My father, stoic in his manner, would examine a piece I had pulled from a pile of driftwood, turn it over, examine it carefully, and then pronounce, "Not this one."

Either the piece of driftwood was too short, or it was too long. It didn't have enough design in the grain of the wood, or it had too much. It was too dark, too stumpy, or too something or other. I felt frustrated and ready to go home.

Finally, after an hour of tromping up and down the beach, my dad stopped and looked closely at a root sticking out of a mound of driftwood. "It's perfect," was his only comment as he took the wood out of the pile of tangled debris and started back towards the car.

I couldn't believe my eyes. The piece of wood was one of the ugliest, oldest, and dirtiest roots I'd ever seen. "Why'd you pick this piece of junk?"

Then it happened: eternal truth sprang forth from a dirty piece of driftwood.

"Dwayne," said my father as he brushed sand from one of the jagged cracks in the root. "You can't look at what the wood is now. You need to see what it can become. Wait and see what I can make from this old root."

I stood on the beach, speechless as my father's words echoed in my mind.

My dad continued down the beach, unaware he had shared a great gem of wisdom that would forever affect my life and ministry. It wasn't until many years later when I was admiring one of his beautiful creations that I would share with him the "Driftwood Principle" I learned that day.

I see this principle reflected in the words God spoke to Samuel when, as the High Priest, Samuel went to anoint the future king of Israel. He was confused when God indicated that none of Jesse's older sons were suited for this role. David, the youngest son and most unlikely candidate for this high position, was God's choice. God said Samuel: "The Lord does not look at the things people look at. People look at the outward appearance, but the Lord looks at the heart." (I Samuel 16:7). Like a rugged piece of driftwood, David was unpolished and unnoticed by his peers, but He was just what God was looking for.

Barnabas: A New Testament Example

Barnabas stands out as one who both knew and lived the "Driftwood Principle." The first time we see Barnabas in the book of Acts, we can imagine him repeating my father's words as he defended Saul of Tarsus:

"You should not look only at who he is now, or who he was in the past. You need to see who he will become. This is a man God is going to use greatly."

The Scriptures don't give us the exact words of the conversation between Barnabas and the Church leaders on the day he brought Saul into their presence. Acts 9:26 says that all of the apostles were afraid of Saul because of his reputation as a zealous persecutor of the Church. They wanted nothing to do with him when he first returned to Jerusalem as a new believer. It was Barnabas who introduced Saul to the council of leaders and paved the way for his future ministry as the apostle to the Gentiles.

There must have been a deep sense of mistrust and uneasiness as Barnabas and Saul walked into the room. Questions and concerns would have been etched on the faces of the apostles as they watched every move of the former persecutor.

What is Barnabas doing with this murderer? Doesn't he know what this guy has done? Has Saul really changed? If not, this is a set-up! Let's get out of here!

Unlike the others in leadership, Barnabas saw beyond who Saul had been to who he would become. God made Barnabas one of the outstanding biblical examples of someone who truly knew how to make disciples. Consider what might have become of Saul of Tarsus if it had not Barnabas. In fact, Barnabas had been Joseph of Cyprus, but he was called Barnabas which means the son of encouragement. He was an literally an "ordinary Joe" whose life made a tremendous impact.

Barnabas also came alongside Mark (also known as John-Mark) and took him under his wing. He did not look at the failures of Mark, but rather saw potential in his younger relative. We do not know how many other people Barnabas influenced in his lifetime. What is undeniable is that he was a man of impact for the Gospel.

The Barnabas Factor Defined

Barnabas impacted his world when he reached out to individuals, influenced them by his example and Christ-like character, and walked alongside them until they reached spiritual maturity. He saw others through God's eyes and was used to touch one person at a time. I call this the "Barnabas Factor." His approach had an impact that reached farther than Barnabas could imagine as his efforts were multiplied in following generations.

There is no doubt that the Church of today needs leaders who go forward with Spirit-led boldness, ministering and preaching the Word of God. It needs those who can influence kings and nations. The Church looks for visionary leaders who will make an impact on the world.

However, today's Church also desperately needs leaders like Barnabas. There is a short supply of men and women who recognize the potential God has placed in others, and mentor them to become the people God wants them to be. There are few who are willing to step back, who will not insist on being the first person listed on the poster. Yet the role of such people is just as important, if not more important, than those who have ministries that resemble that of the Apostle Paul. The Church needs its "unsung heroes" who will allow their character and integrity to speak for itself, and in turn allow their lives to influence others.

God gives these people as a gift to the Church. They are labeled as teachers, mentors, or disciple-makers. Some of them are leaders with a position in front of specific ministries. Others are people who do ordinary things within the ministries of their local churches—perhaps teaching a Sunday School class, or offering their practical service. They have an important role to play within the Body of Christ. Their purpose is to influence others through their life and character. They are like God's beachcombers, able to see a stranger who comes through the church doors with God's eyes.

I am someone like Barnabas. I come alongside others, encouraging them on their journey, and helping them to discover God's gifting and calling for their lives.

For years before I realized this, I tried to be someone I was not intended to be, and as a result I encountered frustration and disillusionment. I wrote my share of resignation letters, thinking a change of job description or location would resolve my situation. It was only when I accepted myself as the person God made me to be—nothing less and nothing more—that I discovered freedom and effectiveness in my efforts to have an impact for God's Kingdom.

Does this sound familiar to you? If so, join me on a journey through the lessons I've learned from the life of Barnabas. I'll tell about the "ordinary Joes" God brought into my life. I'll look at the process God used to help me discover my spiritual gifts and to become comfortable with who He made me to be. I will include details of struggles I faced as I got caught in a performance trap, comparing myself to others. Mentorship principles will be addressed but they are not the focus of this study. I invite you to join me on a journey that encourages ordinary people to have an impact on the world.

Our teacher and mentor on this journey is Barnabas whose impact is not only seen in the pages of the book of Acts, but also in the life and principles taught and lived out by his disciples. His example encourages us to exercise the "Barnabas Factor" in the lives of others, changing the world one life at a time.

You will notice throughout this book that in most cases I refer to the man we often call the Apostle Paul as Saul, his birth name. This follows the biblical pattern, calling him Saul in the events and writing before Acts 13:9, and using the name Paul after that. In a later chapter I will address the circumstances by which he changed his name from the chosen "big guy" Saul, to the servant leader or "little guy" we know as Paul.[1]

The study guide at the end of each chapter is intended for individual or group reflection. It provides an opportunity to apply the principles taught in each chapter to your context or situation. My desire is for readers to carefully and prayerfully consider what God is saying to them through this book. I trust God will use this tool to call an army of men and women who will have an impact upon their world.

I should finish the story which began this introduction, the story about the resignation letter on my desk. That letter ended up in the trash and my thoughts of worthlessness and uncertainty were replaced by purpose and direction after I reached for a study I had done on the life of Barnabas. I asked God to help me see others through His eyes, and to help me make a difference in the world. I realized that the towel in my hand was not to be used to signal surrender, but rather to serve others.

One of the pieces of driftwood my father collected became a clock that now hangs on my living room wall. Through the years many people have commented on its rugged beauty, the incredible designs in the grain of the wood, and the excellent workmanship. My only comment is that it is a work of art and a testimony to someone who could see beyond a dirty, old root—not only looking at what it was, but at what it could become.

CHAPTER 1
FIRST THINGS FIRST

I glanced over my shoulder as I heard footsteps approaching. *Not again! What did I do now?*

Mr. McCaughan, my drafting teacher, came up to my desk. He shook his head as he spoke in a voice which could be heard by the entire class.

"Aye lad," he said. "Let's see what we've got here. Can you tell me what all these squiggles represent?"

I knew he was about to teach the class an important object lesson and that my work would once again be the example of what not to do. I swallowed hard and prepared for the worst. Fortunately his critique always included a suggestion of how I could improve my drawings.

I never expected to learn important life-changing lessons in my high school drafting class, but I got more than I bargained for in those mid-morning sessions. Mr. McCaughan had a way of saying things. His quick quips in his strong Scottish accent stand out in my mind. Highly practical, he taught us the technical skills we needed to draw up plans for everything from simple wooden blocks to complicated house blueprints. I enjoyed his classes, but more importantly, I learned some valuable lessons.

"You rush in where angels fear to tread," he would say when I tackled a project without first thinking through the preliminary steps that needed to be taken.

"If you start well, you'll finish well," he said when he observed I didn't concentrate on drawing the basic structure or shape of an object.

"Make sure you do the first things first, then work on the rest," he would say in reference to following logical patterns of developing a drawing or project. His words of wisdom have served me for much more than drawing cross-sections of a construction project.

I begin our study with one of Mr. McCaughan's insights because there is a need to do the "first things first" and understand *who* the man known as the son of encouragement was before we consider what he did. We must not give in to the temptation to look at his accomplishments and impact without first taking time to consider God's work in his own life.

Some commentators are guilty of this error. They consider Barnabas' relationship with Saul, but overlook significant information that reveals his godly character. This omission leads to a focus on accomplishments, rather than on the life of a person who can be used by God. They forget that the main focus of God's agenda for people is the ongoing transformation of their lives.

At times I've been guilty of putting the last things first in my own life and ministry. For a number of years, I focused on the cold, hard facts: How many people raised their hands at the end of a service? What was the number of teens who attended the youth event? Were baptisms up or down from last year? I felt that measurable statistics were the only way to gauge success.

The result of this led me to a number of incorrect conclusions. I would study the Scriptures, comparing myself with leaders, concluding that I didn't measure up to God's standard. I could not see beyond what a person did. I was on a performance treadmill and I didn't know how to turn it off. I had forgotten to put the first things first, and as a result I found myself frustrated and ready to throw in the towel.

Then God reminded me of a study I had done, now yellowed with years, on the life of Barnabas. I dusted it off and began to understand one of the great secrets of a life which makes an impact for God: who I am as a follower of Christ is more important than what I do for Him.

Barnabas: A Prepared Man

Barnabas comes onto the New Testament stage at a critical point in the history of the early Church. There was a need for authentic leaders during a time when the dynamic growth of the Church, shown in thousands of conversions, pushed the early leadership group to its limit. Barnabas was one of the men who emerged as God's chosen instruments for this task.

God's sovereignty is seen in the background and personal preparation of Barnabas. God used different experiences and valuable lessons which were tailor-made for his personality, equipping him for the specific job God prepared for him to accomplish (Ephesians 2:10).

The exact time when Barnabas came into contact with the disciples is unclear, but it is thought that he was likely a believer during the years Jesus taught and ministered in Palestine. The early Church historian Eusebius identified Barnabas as a member of the group of seventy-two sent out by Jesus to preach the Gospel.[1] This made Barnabas an eyewitness of the life and teachings of Christ. Years later this may have been an important factor in his selection as an envoy of the Jerusalem church to survey the situation in Antioch.

The first clear reference to Barnabas in the Bible is found in Acts 4:36-37. This passage follows a brief description of life among the early group of believers, with a focus on their sharing of possessions to meet the needs of others. Joseph of Cyprus, called Barnabas by the disciples, sold a field he owned and brought the proceeds to the apostles. This brief description gives some insights into the life of the man who would later become an important leader in the Jerusalem church.

Barnabas was a Jew from the island of Cyprus. His ancestors were probably among the people dispersed by the conquering generals who had defeated the Jewish nation. The typical practice of a victorious nation was to forcefully relocate their captives to distant lands in order to squash any hopes of rebellion or independence. For this reason Barnabas' family was among those who lived outside of Judea.

The relocated Jewish community struggled against efforts to be assimilated into the pagan cultures which surrounded them. Synagogues were built in foreign cities to preserve their culture, language, and religious beliefs. The religious leadership in Jerusalem looked down upon this group of Greek or Hellenistic Jews, often treating them as second-class citizens. This was not the mindset of those dispersed, as they took pride in the fact that they remained Jewish in spite of the historic, cultural, and political pressure that enveloped them. They saw themselves as survivors and defenders of the faith.

Barnabas understood and lived within a Greco-Roman cultural background, giving him certain advantages over other early Church leaders. He automatically had something in common with Paul, who came from the Roman outpost city of Tarsus, located in what today is part of eastern Turkey. Growing up in Cyprus gave Barnabas insights into other cultures and languages. He understood the educational system as well as the way of thinking of those who later became his audience. All of these factors, though unknown to him at the time, were factors in his preparation.

Barnabas was a Levite, a fact which gives other important insights into his background and upbringing. The Jewish tribe of Levi had been entrusted with the sacred task of spiritual leadership of the people, and the preservation of the Scriptures. Barnabas learned to read and write in the synagogue. Other Jewish youth did not have the same opportunity to study the Scriptures. This, coupled with the secular education he received, gave him a social position within the Jewish culture, and honed him for future leadership.

Barnabas was a landowner, indicating a high social standing and position within Jewish society. He is not described as a rich landowner, but those who held this position were a part of the middle or upper class. He did not necessarily work the soil, as those who owned land had slaves and paid employees to work their fields or to care for their flocks. Barnabas was part of the administrative middle-class with a social status which helped him develop his leadership skills.

What does the initial statement of Barnabas' background have to do with your life and mine? Perhaps more than you might imagine.

God's preparation and work in our lives does not begin on the day we pray the sinner's prayer. He weaves a series of experiences and factors throughout our lives in order to prepare us for specific tasks or roles. Most of the time we do not give God credit for His hand upon our past, especially as it relates to painful passages. However, as we invest our lives in others, we see that He uses our background to prepare us for specific situations. This enables us to relate to people's problems. This is the sovereignty of God working in our lives.

At times I've looked at my background and thought I didn't have much to offer in service to God. I'm a bus driver's son who spent a good part of my life loving the sport of hockey more than I loved God. At first glance my upbringing doesn't appear very significant, does it?

But God has used my life experiences and love for something other than Him to touch the lives of many others. I was able to encourage João, a bus driver who struggled to keep his family together. I was able to understand André whose dream of playing professional soccer was a stumbling block to making a whole-hearted commitment to Christ. Although I did not know it at the time, God prepared me and built experiences into my life so I would be able to touch others.

Barnabas: A Transformed Man

The description of Barnabas as a Levite from Cyprus who sold a field and gave the money to the disciples is only one of the characteristics which causes him to stand out from other people in the Jerusalem church. The character qualities in the life of Barnabas reveal a man who was transformed by the power of God.

According to Old Testament law and customs, Levites were not allowed to own land, but rather were to depend on God for their provisions.[2] Jewish leaders had strayed from this principle, and historians tell us that the Levites were among the richest people of their day.

Was Luke trying to tell us something in this description of Barnabas? I believe he was, as his readers would understand the conversion of a Levite to be a miracle. The sale of his land and gift offered to the poor testified to a transformed life. This act set Barnabas apart and consecrated him for service, something intended for all Levites. It opened new opportunities of service to God, as Barnabas was freed from the responsibilities of the administration of his workers and care of the land.

God may not ask us to sell all we have and give the proceeds to the poor, but He asks each person to make significant choices which reflect a submitted and transformed heart. This is part of God's work in our lives as He takes us through a process of molding and forming us into the image of Christ.

The transformation of Barnabas is noted from the very moment he is introduced to New Testament readers. Known as the "son of encouragement," his name is an indication of his character. The King James translation of the New Testament opts for the words "son of consolation" to describe Barnabas. Luke used the Greek word *parakleseos* to describe Barnabas. It comes from the same root word Jesus used when He promised another "Comforter," identified as the Holy Spirit (John 14:26; 16:7). It is no coincidence that a man who would later be described as "being a good man, full of the Holy Spirit" (Acts 11:24) would possess spiritual qualities which gave him a ministry of encouragement and comfort.

We are not told the circumstances leading to the use of the "son of encouragement" nickname, but we do know Barnabas' character and gifts as a mentor only serve to reinforce this description. Barnabas was one who came alongside churches and individuals to help them in their spiritual growth. He put others first and was used by God in the lives of many people within the early Church.

The description of the attitudes of Barnabas and others in the early Church are directly contrasted with the deception of Ananias and Sapphira who attempted to use the sale of a parcel of their land to gain recognition and praise (Acts 5:1-10).

While Barnabas sold his property and gave the money to the church out of pure and upright motives, Ananias and Sapphira were not of noble character. This taught Luke's readers that a person's motivation in doing the right thing is more important than the act itself. What matters to God is the heart attitude in which any service or gift is offered. True to this day, the standard by which God measures a person's deeds is a transformed life and not any acts of benevolence.

The second mention of Barnabas in the New Testament serves to underline the importance of his integrity and character. His reputation grew during the period between the first mention of his name in Acts 4:36 and the second mention of his name in Acts 9:27. Accepted and recognized as a trustworthy man, Barnabas was able to present Saul to the leadership of the church in Jerusalem. It was through his recommendation that Saul was given an opportunity to be heard.

What is not said about Barnabas in this passage speaks volumes. There is no mention of him being afraid to take a risk by presenting a murderer to the council. Not a word is spoken of the conversations he had with Saul before this event, probably under the watchful eye of others who would not give Saul a hearing.

Barnabas is described as a person willing to give a person a second chance. He must have been encouraged by the reception afforded to Saul. The leaders showed an appreciation of his miraculous conversion. They gave Saul the freedom to speak in public, something he did with boldness and effectiveness. Barnabas would later reflect on this as he considered a partner for the work in Antioch.

Unfortunately the warm welcome extended to Saul by the apostles was not shared by all. The ensuing debate resulted in attempts to take Saul's life. He was encouraged by the Jerusalem believers to pack his bags and head home while things cooled down.

The third reference to Barnabas in the New Testament is found in Acts 11:22-24. As a trusted messenger sent out from the Jerusalem church leaders, Barnabas found himself thrust into his first key ministry role in a foreign city.

The persecution which followed Stephen's martyrdom caused the dispersion of believers to the Roman territories of Phoenicia, Cyprus, and Antioch (Acts 7:1 – 8:1a). Luke makes particular mention of men from Cyprus and Cyrene who went to Antioch and preached the Gospel. This resulted in a great number of people turning to the Lord. Barnabas, who also came from Cyprus, was chosen to go and assess the situation.

The choice of Barnabas as the man to investigate the happenings in Antioch speaks of his character. He had won the trust of leadership and had proven himself through difficult times of persecution. This qualified him to care for and shepherd the emerging group.

Upon his arrival at Antioch, Barnabas showed himself to be a man who observed things before passing judgment. He did not come into the group at Antioch with a preconceived notion of what was happening, nor with a message from the Jerusalem leadership. His first task was to observe the evidence of God's grace at work in the lives of the believers and to go on from there. This reveals his great patience and quiet confidence in God.

The immediate ministry role in which Barnabas engaged himself was to encourage those around him to remain true to God with all their heart. Once again his "son of encouragement" nickname describes the ministry he would have in Antioch. There were those among the group who had fled the persecution in Jerusalem and who sensed they had failed the Lord. Other Gentile believers in the group were uncertain about how they would be accepted by Jewish leadership. The ministry of Barnabas was to stimulate this diverse group to be faithful and true to the Lord.

The high point of the description of Barnabas' character is found in Acts 11:24 where he is called a "good man, full of the Holy Spirit and faith." Much like Stephen and the seven elders chosen to serve the church (Acts 6:1-4), the character quality which stands out in Barnabas is his spirituality.

That Barnabas is called a "good man, filled with the Holy Spirit" speaks of his personal integrity and character. Goodness was a by-product of the filling of the Holy Spirit in his life. He demonstrated the fruit of the Spirit, reflecting God's nature. People noted the difference in the way he lived. The presence of the Holy Spirit in his life became the characteristic which influenced all he said or did. Like a crown jewel in the list of his qualities, the filling of the Holy Spirit made Barnabas a man used by God.

This factor is the single most important aspect in any success Barnabas experienced in his personal ministry. His influence upon others came from a life touched by the indwelling presence of Christ through the Holy Spirit. The "Barnabas Factor" (which I define as influencing a person towards Christ-likeness) flowed from the fact that Barnabas had first been touched by the Master Discipler.

It is only after the description of Barnabas' character and emphasis on his spiritual qualities that Luke gives readers a description of what he did: "A great number of people were brought to the Lord" (Acts 11:24) through his ministry. Fruitfulness in Barnabas' ministry was not the focus of what Luke relayed to his readers, but rather the natural consequence of a life transformed by God.

Could it be that, in a world of instant gratification and quick-fix solutions, we as Christians get some things backwards? Today's Church places emphasis on results, often neglecting the areas of personal character and integrity. Christians go from conference to conference seeking new methods or formulas for success. Much of our literature is concerned with how to resolve issues and problems, providing easy three-step outlines for everything a pastor or leader desires to accomplish. "Ministry" is not gauged so much by who we are, but rather by what we do. It would seem we have forgotten to do the "first things first."

Eunice Smith, a missionary colleague, says in response to these ideas:

I have often seen this syndrome—striving to reach goals—attempting to get results with a specific scheme or strategy that worked for someone else; energy and money spent on attending seminars on methodology, a different idea every month or so. We all use a method, and can learn from each other, but it's the frantic emphasis on the "how to" and nervous analysis of results that I have found disturbing. We too easily forget that God wants to work in us, while or even before He works through us. [3]

Those who want to make a lasting impact for the Kingdom of God need to focus on the right things. Character is more important than achievement. Personal integrity is more important than abilities or methods.

The life of Barnabas teaches us that a life of impact flows from being a man or woman of godly character. No amount of activity or title can give this distinction to a leader. Rather, it is the process God uses in each and every individual who chooses to make a difference in the world.

This truth is clearly pointed out by author J. Robert Clinton in *The Making of a Leader*. Talking about the process God uses to call and develop a leader, Clinton states: "Integrity is foundational for effective leadership; it must be instilled early in a leader's character." [4] Clinton also goes on to say: "Character is foundational if a leader is to influence people for God's purposes." [5]

God uses the experiences of our lives to develop our understanding of His word, our integrity, and what it means to obey Him. His primary concern is to shape our character and to produce Christ-like followers.

This holds true in the example of Barnabas. He is known as a man of godly character, not for his position, nor for what he did in the Church but because he was "a good man, full of the Holy Spirit and faith." His personal integrity would influence those who became his disciples. It is clearly this characteristic, putting the first things first, which made Barnabas a person of lasting impact.

Study Guide

ACTIVE LEARNING ...

In groups of two or three, complete the following assignment and then present your work to the larger group. (If doing this study on your own, you can write your answers on two separate pages of paper.)

1. Prepare a 30-second television commercial which advertises a seminar on effective Christian ministry. Identify the needs your seminar will address as well as three tools it will offer to participants. Include all the glitter of a Hollywood production.

2. Prepare a 30-second television commercial, this time advertising a weekend retreat of spiritual renewal which emphasizes fasting and prayer. Express the benefits of such a weekend, focusing on character development and life transformation.

After each group has presented their commercials, consider the following questions:

1. Which commercial was easier to prepare?

2. Which commercial would be best received in today's Christian community?

CONSIDER ...

Read Acts 4:36-37 and 11:22-24. Respond to the following questions:

1. What aspects of the background of Barnabas prepared him for God's mission in his life? Make a list of the ways each quality equipped him for his future ministry.

2. What are the character qualities in the life of Barnabas which strike you as most important in these passages? Is the focus of Luke's description the fruitfulness of his ministry or his godly character?

3. Read Galatians 5:22-24. How does the fruit of the Spirit compare to Barnabas' character and personality?

RESPOND ...

Principle: Mentorship is the process by which one person influences others toward Christ-likeness, flowing from who they are as a followers of Jesus Christ and not from what they do for Him.

1. In what ways does the above principle apply to the life of Barnabas?

2. Why are we tempted to focus on the results of the life of a person and not on their character? What are God's priorities in the lives of His followers?

3. What is one way you can develop a deeper sense of Christ-likeness in your life? What steps can you take to accomplish this task?

CHAPTER 2
SOMEONE'S KNOCKING AT THE DOOR

It was a cold, rainy, miserable winter night. I was glad I had no appointments and could be home with my family. A fire glowed in our fireplace, warming our Porto Alegre home which, like most Brazilian houses, had no central heating. We checked the television to see if there was anything worth watching. Each of our family members vied for a spot near the fireplace.

Then someone at our front gate began clapping loudly. He wasn't clapping because he enjoyed the show we were watching. It was the Brazilian custom to clap outside a gate instead of knocking on a door. (It also may have been because our doorbell didn't work.)

"*Tio*," called a young boy, drenched in the rain. "*Tio!*"

How I hate being called 'uncle' at times like this, I thought to myself as I went to the door.

"How can I help you?" I called out. I stood under the cover of the overhang which protected the entrance to our house.

"Do you have any food you can give me?"

"Just a minute," I said as I ducked back into the warmth and dryness of our home.

"Who is it?" asked my wife. "What do they want?"

"It's a boy asking for food. Do we have anything we can give him? Does anyone know where I left my raincoat?"

Within a few minutes my wife had put together some leftovers and bread from the cupboard. "Poor thing," she said as she put the items into a plastic bag.

Both my children looked out the window and tried to guess the boy's age. They scolded me for not asking him to come under the cover of our front porch. They noticed he was wearing a soaked T-shirt. My only concern was to find my raincoat so I could give the boy his package and get back to my warm, comfortable home.

When I handed the boy the bag of food, he flashed a broad smile. As he looked over its contents he spoke again. "Thank you, *tio*," he said. "No one else will give me anything. Can I come back some other time?"

Not sure how to answer him, I asked a question of my own. "*Como se chama?*" "What's your name?"

The boy grinned broadly and replied, "Luis Alberto."

"You can come back, Luis. But you should go home and get out of this rain."

"*Muito obrigado, tio!*" "Thank you!"

Water soaked into my shoes and I wiped the raindrops from my glasses. I smiled as I watched him walk off. This time I didn't mind him calling me uncle.

That was our first contact with Luis Alberto. During his subsequent visits we discovered he was the oldest child of a family of seven. His father had abandoned the family and his mother no longer had enough food for all the children. As the oldest he was sent out to fend for himself.

One evening we were getting ready to go to the children's program at our church. As we walked out the door Luis Alberto appeared. My children were on a first-name basis with him by now, and invited him to come along. That night we entered a new phase in our relationship with Luis Alberto. He accepted Christ into his life through the children's club, and our church began to reach out to his family.

I learned an important lesson on that cold, rainy night when Luis Alberto walked into my life: you never know when the knock at the door might be a person sent by God.

I like to think that the first encounter of Barnabas with Saul was similar to the night I met Luis Alberto. I imagine it could have taken place on a cold, rainy, miserable night.

The details of the first meeting between Barnabas and Saul are unknown. We don't know if Barnabas greeted Saul with a welcoming embrace or a polite handshake. We are not told whether he showed any reservations as he was introduced to the man who was known for his active persecution of the Church. They may have already been acquaintances as they shared a common bond as Jews who lived outside of Jerusalem and Israel. What is certain is that their relationship became one of the best examples of discipleship and mentoring the New Testament offers.

The Divine Selection Process

Scripture is clear: God wants His followers to make disciples. While the Great Commission of Matthew 28:18-20 is often taught in the context of world missions, its implications are for all Christians, regardless of their vocation or location. We are to proclaim the name of Christ and to lead people to a life transformed by His power. We are to make an impact on the world, a task often accomplished one life at a time.

Does this mean we should all abandon our jobs and buy a one-way ticket to Botswana? Who decides where to go? Who chooses the people we are to influence or disciple? Are there any cut-and-dried answers to these questions?

I believe the relationship between Barnabas and Saul gives us insight into these questions. While there were many candidates who could have become his disciple, Barnabas chose to invest his life into Saul's. This selection followed a purposeful and deliberate pattern as Barnabas made his impact for God.

Who has God brought into your life?

God brings people into our lives with His purposes in mind. Some of these He uses to shape and mold our character. Others He brings to us so we can influence them and help them along in their relationship with the Lord. Our part is to observe those around us, prayerfully consider the role we would play in their lives, and practice patience and perseverance as we impart our lives to them.

The first reference which indicates any relationship between Barnabas and Saul is found in Acts 9:27, when Barnabas brought Saul before the apostles. Barnabas acted as a peacemaker and go-between. This event, according to Galatians 1:18, took place three years after Saul's dramatic conversion on the road to Damascus. After leaving Damascus he had been in Arabia. Those in Jerusalem heard of his conversion and were skeptical of his motives. Their reluctance to give Saul a hearing was only broken when one of their own, a man of confidence and integrity, stood up on Saul's behalf and brought him into their presence.

Initially the relationship between Barnabas and Saul is not well-defined. They seem to be mere acquaintances. Most likely Barnabas spoke to Saul or heard him preach before he took the risk of presenting him to the apostles. Saul made an impression upon Barnabas as he boldly proclaimed the name of Christ in the streets of Jerusalem. Following these events the two went their separate ways, as Saul was shuffled off to Tarsus for his own protection while Barnabas remained in Jerusalem.

It was not until years later that Barnabas sought Saul to help in the growing church in Antioch (Acts 11:25-26). We do not know whether Saul was in a holding pattern, working in the family tent business, or whether he was actively preaching the Gospel in Tarsus. Apparently Saul did not need a great deal of convincing to join forces with Barnabas, as he packed up his bags and set off for Antioch without delay. But the seeds of a deeper relationship were planted in Jerusalem when Barnabas brought Saul before the leaders.

This was not a purely passive process, as Barnabas' observations needed to lead to actions. He was pro-active and purposeful as he sought out Saul. Barnabas paid attention and knew where to find Saul. He saw potential in Saul and acted upon it. Barnabas showed initiative and leadership as he invited Saul to join him to be his apprentice. Like a tool in the hands of God, Barnabas would be used to shape and form Saul's character.

Often the people God wants me to influence are not far from me. They can be members of my family, church, or neighborhood. My experience is that I don't have to go out looking for disciples, but rather I need to be attentive to those around me. As I develop relationships with them and observe their needs or abilities, I am naturally drawn to some who desire to learn from me and to spend time together. God places these people in my life with His specific purpose in mind.

The Greek word *oikos*, commonly translated as house or home, can also be used to describe our sphere of influence or acquaintances.[1] This ever-changing group of people includes those who exercise their influence upon us, as well as those in whom we can invest our lives. Some of these people are friends we've known for years, while others are relative strangers who have recently come into our lives. Our personal *oikos* is a great source of resources to shape us or be shaped by us.

Barnabas followed a simple process as he considered his options to discover a partner for the ministry in Antioch. After assessing the needs around him, he observed who was available and suited for the task. He acted upon his observations and set out to Tarsus to invite Saul.

Who are the people God wants you to influence? They may be closer than you think, making up a part of the natural network of your relationships. He places individuals in your life with a purpose, either to shape you through them, or for you to have an impact upon their lives. Quite likely there are two or three people who come to your mind as you read this.

God's Confirmation through Prayer

Although not implicit in the Scriptural accounts of Barnabas' decision to seek out and invite Saul, his selection process was undoubtedly complemented with prayer. Barnabas not only knew who he should seek as his partner, but also knew what he would do with Saul once they began their mutual ministry (Acts 13:1-3; 14:23).

What we know of Barnabas' character and personality points to a man who enjoyed an intimate relationship with the Lord. In many other instances he sought God's leading and guidance on his knees. It would not be out of character for Barnabas to bathe this decision in prayer, as his ministry and influence upon others flowed from a deep personal walk with the Lord.

Jesus followed a similar pattern as He took steps to select His disciples. Jesus chose His inner circle of followers from a fairly large group of acquaintances. He spent a full night in prayer before making the final selection of the twelve (Luke 6:12-16). No doubt He put much thought into this decision, consulting His Father before calling those God would use to spread the Gospel.

The twelve men who emerged as Jesus' disciples were an unlikely group, a mixture of rugged fishermen, hated tax collectors, and nobodies. I can imagine Jesus shook his head and wondered if this group was ever going to "get it" as they fought among each other to see who would be the greatest. They came up with odd questions, revealing their numbness to the things of God. They were common men who were not part of the crowd one would expect to be leadership material. They were not the cream of the crop, but Jesus invested His life into them because the Father had revealed His will through prayer that this was the group God would use to turn the world upside down.

In December 1980 I returned "home" after spending six months attending the Capernwray Bible School in Austria. I came back with a keen desire to be involved in the ministry of my local church. I prayed for God to guide me to two or three people I could disciple. My challenge was that "home" was now a different city as my family had moved while I was away, and my church was full of strangers. I had no idea what God would do or how He would lead. Perhaps that's why I prayed so earnestly.

God answered my prayers. The church we now attended was smaller than our previous church, and there were few candidates to consider. There were two young teenagers, Mark and Brad, who displayed a desire to grow in their relationship with the Lord. As I continued to pray, the two kept showing up in my life, involved with me in one way or another.

I began to spend more time with Mark and Brad. As our relationship developed they became my good friends, mountain-climbing partners, and closest disciples. Others came into my life, but the impact and influence which marks my personal ministry began to flourish during the years we spent together. To this day, even though we live thousands of miles apart, they are among my best friends.

God tends to work in our lives in this way. Once we submit ourselves to His will, we discover that He directs our paths to intersect with others who need a helping hand or an example to follow. As we look around us and as we pray for His guidance, there is no shortage of people who need someone to help them along in their relationship with God.

Those God brings into our lives may surprise us. He often takes ordinary people and transforms them into His chosen and approved vessels. Paul candidly states that God chooses the weak things of this world so His greatness and power can be revealed to the world (2 Corinthians 12:10). In this way it is God who is glorified, not the vessel He uses to accomplish His purposes.

Our Part: Risk, Time, and Patience

Once we have looked around us and prayerfully considered who God wants us to influence, we must consider three vital ingredients of mentorship. They make up the "Barnabas Factor" in a person's life.

The first ingredient in the partnership between Barnabas and Saul was risk. Barnabas had no guarantee that his investment in Saul's life would bear fruit. Many in Jerusalem would not have pinned their hopes upon a former persecutor, but Barnabas saw beyond Saul's past and pressed ahead with his plan.

Disciple-making involves taking risks. The time and energy it takes to get to know a person and to let them get to know you are resources no one wants to squander on a sure failure. That is where God comes in, as sometimes those the world would pronounce as failures are the people with whom God wants us to work. There are times when God directs us to people who come from unlikely backgrounds. They may not be individuals who stand out in a crowd, nor those who speak eloquently, but they have a pure heart and want to serve God.

The second important aspect or characteristic in the development of a solid mentoring relationship is time. There is no substitute in God's training process for time. Many lessons cannot be learned during a weekend seminar. Like a rough diamond in its refining stages, we need to rub shoulders with others who help us and teach us from their lives. This is an essential part of the maturing and character-building process God uses in our lives.

There is a temptation to read the book of Acts and think Luke's timeline of the life of Saul is as short as the chapters. Acts 8 introduces Saul as a vicious persecutor. He is converted on the road to Damascus in Acts 9. Two chapters later, he becomes a partner with Barnabas in Antioch. In Acts 13, Barnabas and Saul are sent out on the first missionary journey. All of the events seem to pass by quickly as we read the progression of events in Saul's life.

But Galatians 2:1 indicates that fourteen years had passed between the first introduction of Saul to Church leaders in Acts 9:36-37 and the time he and Barnabas returned to Jerusalem.[2] Saul would have learned many lessons during this time, as he spent three to five years in ministry with Barnabas in Antioch and on their missionary travels. This differs from the popular belief in a fast-track approach to ministry preparation. Saul's mentorship was not a process like a quick microwave-oven, but rather more like that of a slow wood-burning oven.

I'm not a patient person. "Rushing in where angels fear to tread" describes my life and is a characteristic which marks me to this day. When God called me to serve Him in missions, I wanted to get onto a plane and head out—yesterday. I struggled with the mission policies which impeded my immediate release to the harvest fields, as they required years of education and ministry experience. I didn't have time for all of that!

However, I now see how every experience in my life worked to help me mature and to prepare me for my future. In my formative years I was introduced to godly men and women who left an imprint upon my life. My education gave me important ministry tools I did not previously possess. My preparation was something ordained by God. There is also no replacement for time spent with others who have cast their shadow upon my life and influenced me towards Christ-likeness.

Related to the aspect of time, the third ingredient for a productive mentorship is patience. You cannot give up on those God brings into your life. Spiritual growth takes perseverance. Our disciples will make mistakes and will disappoint us. They are as human and sinful as we are. If your relationship to them is not salted with patience, you will be disappointed.

Barnabas exercised patience as he watched and worked with Saul. Anyone who has spent years working together with another knows this is how it works. Perhaps this lesson later inspired Paul when he penned the words of Philippians 1:6, reminding his hearers of his confidence that God would complete the good work He began in the lives of His followers.

When I think of the patience needed to disciple a person, a number of people come to mind. One of them is Thomas.[3]

I was at a team meeting at seminary where we divided up students for our mentorship program. Our process was like picking teams for a game of sandlot baseball: "I want him!" "You get him!" "No, you take so-and-so!" There wasn't much spirituality involved in the selection process.

I ended up with Thomas. While others breathed a sigh of relief, I shook my head. *Not him! He's got so many problems! Why does it have to be me?* All of these thoughts flooded my mind and I felt sorry for myself.

It would be a lie to say that everything went well with this young man. It was difficult to find times and places to meet together. Often he showed up late, or didn't show up at all. He didn't always agree with or finish the tasks assigned to him. The many inconsistencies in his life seemed to indicate he was not fit for ministry.

There were times I felt like giving up. If we had been in the sporting world, I would have traded him for "future considerations," but that was something God would not allow.

One day, after a year of meeting together, something clicked. The person who came into my office had a different attitude. Something had changed. Thomas was now willing to deal with key issues and to seek God's power for victory in areas of temptation. The transformation which took place changed my attitude toward Thomas, and I began to see him through different eyes. Today he and his wife are members of a pastoral team.

Others asked me what I had done to help this young man. The only answer I could offer was that I didn't give up on him. I was too ashamed to admit I had seriously thought about doing that very thing, but in the end was glad I had not. Patience had paid its dividends.

This brings me back full circle to the aspect of prayer. When I offer myself to God to be a tool in His hands, I need to be in constant communion and trust Him to direct my steps. I must trust that He will bring people into my life to influence and disciple. I must be confident that He will do His work, in His timing, in the people of His choosing. I must pray and ask for wisdom, faithfulness, and *stickablity*[4] in the process of seeing a person molded into the image of Christ.

As you open yourself to God's command to make disciples, you are faced with a number of questions or issues. You need to look around and see who the people might be, seek God's confirmation in prayer, and be willing to risk the time needed for character development in their lives. You need to be patient and to trust God to use you as a sharpening tool in the lives of your disciples.

The question at hand is not whether you are willing to be used by God, nor if you want to please Him. The real issue is whether you will allow God, in His wisdom and sovereignty, to choose those whom He places in your life. Often the circumstances by which these people come to you are not of your design. They might even show up on a cold, rainy night. God may direct an antagonistic and vicious persecutor of the Church, feared and rejected by others, into your life. In all of this it is important to remember that you never know if the person who knocks at your door is someone sent by God.

Study Guide

ACTIVE LEARNING …

In groups of two or three, complete the following activities and then present your work to the larger group. (Individuals can write their lists on two separate pages of paper.)

1. Make a list of the five most important qualities you look for in a person into whom you invest your life and time. In an ideal situation, what would be your expectations of a new disciple?

2. Make a list of five reasons why the Jerusalem leaders feared and did not trust Saul. How would you describe their preconceived notion of him?

After compiling the two lists, consider the following questions:

3. Would you have considered Saul as a potential disciple or person into whom you'd invest hours—perhaps years—of your life? Why or why not?

4. What might a modern-day Saul look like? Under what circumstances might he or she come into your life?

CONSIDER …

Read Mark 3:13-19, Luke 5:1-11 and Luke 5:27-32. Answer the following questions:

1. What possible character defects can you identify in the men Jesus chose to be his closest followers? Did their defects disqualify them from this high calling?

2. What can we learn from Jesus in His selection of the twelve disciples?

3. Compare the calling of Saul (Acts 9:1-31) to that of Jesus' disciples. What are the similarities in their calling? What were the positive character traits that Jesus and Barnabas saw in the lives of their disciples?

25

RESPOND ...

Principle: Mentoring or discipleship involve perseverance and commitment to faithfully influence those who God has placed in my life.

1. How does the above principle apply to the life of Barnabas?

2. Who are the people God has placed in your personal *oikos* or sphere of influence?

3. What are the circumstances that God used to bring you together?

Take time to pray for these people, asking God to give you discernment, insight and perseverance as you influence these people towards Christ-likeness.

CHAPTER 3
AN INVITATION TO THOSE WHO CAN'T SWING A HAMMER

I was in one of my obnoxious, adolescent moods. (Perhaps, my mother would add, one of my *many* obnoxious, adolescent moods.)

The phone rang and I grabbed the receiver before anyone else could get to it. "Hello, City Morgue. You stab 'em, we slab 'em. The good ones go to heaven and the bad ones go to...hello!" was my rehearsed greeting. I pretended I didn't see the disapproving glare my mother threw in my direction.

Without missing a beat the person on the other end of the line disguised his voice and replied, "This is your Aunt Martha and that's the rudest thing I have ever heard from anyone your age. You ought to be ashamed of yourself!"

I was taken back and unsure how to respond as I stuttered. "Um, well, I...wait, I don't have an Aunt Martha! Who is this?"

The laugh on the other line gave away the person's identity. It was Tim Tjosvold, our church's new youth pastor.

"Oh, it's only you. What can I do for you? Do you want to speak to my mother?"

Tim had tried to talk with me on a number of occasions. I was an outside observer and not a participant in the life of the youth group. I knew he wanted me to get involved at church, but I had other priorities.

"I was just wondering if you could help me," Tim said. "As you know, we're working on a youth choir production through the fall and I was..."

"I'm not a singer," I said, hoping to cut the conversation short.

"Not everyone is, but I was wondering if you might help me with something else. There's a great deal of drama in the production and ..."

27

"I'm not an actor either," I interrupted him a second time. There was a pause on the other end of the line.

"We also need someone to help out with props and a few other odd jobs. Would you be willing to swing a hammer with me for a couple of Saturday afternoons to help make a small stage?"

I was the last person in the world who should have been invited to swing a hammer. Tim was probably the second-last person who should have been handling this task. We're both "handyman-challenged."

But I couldn't think of an excuse to back out of Tim's request. I soon found myself committed to work with him.

The time spent during those two Saturday afternoons accomplished more than making a small, precarious stage. In spite of many bent nails and hours of frustration, we became friends. This was the beginning of a relationship with a man of God who impacted my life. In fact, Tim Tjosvold became one of the most influential people in my life, as his love for God and zest for life were contagious.

The initial step of the relationship between Barnabas and Saul reveals a commitment to relational ministry. While what they did together is often spiritualized, there is no doubt that the first year of their ministry in Antioch served to develop and deepen their relationship. Together they taught and ministered to the believers in Antioch, a task that built trust and companionship between the two men.

Saul was a great help to Barnabas, but that was not the only reason he was included on the ministry team. Prior to Saul's arrival, Barnabas had had a fruitful ministry that resulted in many people coming to the faith. The key element was not what the two would do in their time together, but rather the relationship that would develop.

The highly relational aspect of Barnabas' ministry with Saul reveals his secret to effectiveness. Up to this point Saul had ministered and preached in isolation from others. Now, for the first time he would work together with Barnabas. They sharpened their gifts, abilities, and teamwork. The operative feature in all of this is that they were *together*.

Relational ministry is the term I use to describe what Barnabas did with Saul. Barnabas was a master of this concept as he imparted his life to others. This became a way of life that permeated all he did as he made his impact for God.

I'd like to make four comparisons to help deepen our understanding of the concept of relational ministry, especially as it refers to a mentor and his disciples. The comparisons flow from observations of the life and ministry of Barnabas, but also take into account the principles I learned while swinging a hammer on those Saturday afternoons. Some of them do not deal with "either-or" issues, but rather reflect an order of priorities.

Personal versus Programmed

One of the wisest things Barnabas did was to seek out and invite Saul to join the ministry team in Antioch. The two men spent much time together, working, praying, and developing a deep relationship. The partnership they formed is an example of the positive results and impact that relational ministry can reap.

The fundamental principle modeled by Barnabas in his mentorship of Saul is the personal attention and friendship developed with his disciple. The act of traveling to Tarsus and seeking out Saul speaks for itself, as Barnabas showed interest and saw potential in the life of this man. The invitation to work in Antioch indicated a commitment to work together and to develop their relationship.

Barnabas did not have a structured yearly plan or a set of neatly packaged lessons when he set out to find Saul. A handful of principles he had learned and wanted to impart into the life of others guided him. He also realized he would be enriched and his ministry multiplied in a partnership with Saul.

In today's way of thinking, the example of Barnabas doesn't give us much on which to base a discipleship program. He doesn't give us something that is easily copied. He left no manual or booklet of effective leadership principles. Barnabas leaves us with one basic principle: when a godly person spends time with eager learners, there is bound to be a lasting impact made upon their lives.

This does not mean there is no place for structured mentorship programs or studies. There are many fine materials developed to aid believers who desire to grow in their life and service for God. There are a number of methods leaders can use to deepen the walk of their disciples with the Lord. There is no lack of good material that can be used to accomplish this task.

However, the key element to any mentoring process is the formation of relationships that influence others towards Christ-like character. The material studied or the program used can be an important tool in this process, but it is not the wood that fuels the fire. The examples of great men or women of faith, together with their writings, may encourage and inspire others in their journey, but they do not replace a mentor who walks with them. A ministry task can be tackled in the training of younger leaders, but this is not the focus of discipleship. No program or methodology can take the place of relationships, as the goal is to influence others towards Christ-likeness. This is best done within the context of contact with godly people.

I have personally benefited from Bible studies, special programs and seminars. I've accumulated biblical knowledge and learned life-changing principles from godly men and women as they used these tools to train me. God has used a number of authors to teach me valuable lessons. I am a richer person for my involvement in these activities.

I've also learned a great deal from the time I've spent hammering nails, cleaning corrals, or being involved in menial tasks while accompanied by a godly person. As I've rubbed shoulders with these men and women of God, something has rubbed off on me.

This confirms the principle that our influence upon others flows from who we are, not what we do. Relational ministry affirms and emphasizes the personal element. It may use study guides or programs as tools in the process of leading a person towards spiritual maturity, but it recognizes the danger of thinking that mentorship can be programmed into a series of lessons or experiences without deep relationships. It acknowledges that someone who has completed a class or structured program does not necessarily become a true follower of Christ.

Paul Ens, a missionary colleague, says: "Information without transformation leads to deception."[1] I would add that information or programmed learning without godly relationships magnifies this negative result, and leads to shallow, ineffective followers of Christ. This underlines the need for biblical truth to be exemplified in a teacher or mentor, resulting in an impact upon their hearers that develops Christ-like character.

Intentional versus Haphazard

For some readers, a personal approach to ministry may imply a haphazard or poorly planned administration of time and resources. The example of Barnabas gives no basis or foundation to this assertion, but rather indicates an intentional application of his influence upon the life of Saul. The purposeful inclusion of Saul in Barnabas' life and ministry was not circumstantial, nor was Saul a random selection as Barnabas' partner.

Barnabas specifically sought out Saul, making a special effort to travel to Tarsus to extend an invitation to his future partner. Why did he do so?

Their previous experience in Jerusalem formed the basis for their relationship. Barnabas took the initiative on this occasion and brought Saul before the Church leaders. There is no reason to believe they were acquainted beforehand, but this single event represents the sowing of seeds of trust and the beginnings of a deep relationship. Barnabas then observed the freedom and boldness Saul exhibited in his preaching ministry that followed his acceptance by leaders. He took a mental note for possible future reference of where Saul was sent by the apostles.

Barnabas sought out Saul to complement his ministry, adding a new element to the existing group of believers in Antioch. Barnabas was not alone in Antioch as a group of Christians was formed before his arrival. Either Barnabas was convinced that Saul would enrich the group with his personal ministry, or he was aware that Antioch would present an opportunity in which Saul could develop. Perhaps both were the case.

The example of Barnabas' intentional relationship with Saul did not include a set curriculum or an established program. It was initiated with the purpose of developing character and ministry skills. It was the product of time spent in prayer in the selection process. It included a definite invitation that required action on the part of Saul to follow and submit himself to Barnabas' leadership. Although at first it included a well-defined ministry task, it was flexible and responded to the moving of the Holy Spirit to take the Gospel to new regions.

Character development is the goal of relational ministry and a mentoring relationship today. Although a common task or project can be included, it is not the focus of the time spent together. Teaching ministry skills may also be an aspect that is included in the process, but it too is not the reason to be together. The primary objective is to aid those whom God has placed into our lives to know Christ and to become more like Him.

A mentoring relationship needs to be intentional and not haphazardly thrown together. Once we have established the people God would have us influence, we need to be deliberate in our actions and focus on the objective of developing Christ-like character in their lives. This may include the use of a tool or program that facilitates the teaching of important information or the imparting of useful ministry skills. As Paul succinctly states in Philippians 3:10, the goal is to know Christ and become like Him.

Equipping versus Imparting

The terms equipping and imparting are often used as synonyms, but they have an entirely distinct focus. While they are both an important part of the mentoring process, the goal to equip others for effective service takes precedence over the teaching of specific material or curriculum. This is the case in the example of Barnabas and Saul.

Barnabas' invitation to Saul included an element of preparation or equipping for ministry. This was done while working together and learning skills. It was not just a case of passing along knowledge or information, but practical know-how. Their time was spent in the streets and at the homes of people, not in a classroom or formal setting. They touched the lives of real people and had to deal with tough issues in a church full of new converts.

This environment was a greenhouse for growth, producing fruit in the lives of both men. It provided Saul with a structure and basis for ministry he had not developed on his own. Barnabas sharpened his abilities as a mentor, learning to share his responsibilities and encouraging Saul to hone his skills. Both emerged as stronger, well-rounded leaders from time spent together.

The best way to get needed experience and preparation is to work together with someone who can "show us the ropes." Barnabas was willing to be that person for Saul. It involved more than sharing information, and included ministering side-by-side, learning as they went. There is no doubt Saul's knowledge of the life of Christ grew, but the focus of his time with Barnabas was to develop character and ministry skills.

Many seminaries and Christian schools could learn from this example. Ministry formation includes more than packing information into the brain of a young candidate and declaring that their years of education suit them for ministry. Churches are permeated with pastors or workers who have all the head knowledge they need to write volumes of theological literature, but have no idea how to put into practice the "nuts and bolts" to help a person who comes to their office. All too often they have entered the pastorate with books on their shelves and certificates on their walls, but with little or no hands-on experience of dealing with the problems of real people. They have not walked alongside nor spent time with a "Barnabas."

Barnabas used a ministry task as a tool in the process that provided Saul with the practical experience he needed. His invitation was for Saul to come and learn as they ministered together. Barnabas taught a great deal as he included Saul in the daily activities as pastor of a growing congregation. Later their relationship would develop into a partnership where Saul was in the forefront of their activities. Eventually it ended with Saul embarking as the leader of his own ministry team.

I have used drama as a discipleship tool in my ministry. A group of young people formed a drama team. Each member was taught skills for our evangelistic presentation and for practical ministry. In the process of preparing a drama, we would study together, pray together, learn evangelism skills, and develop a relationship which went deeper than our final performance. Accountability structures were put into place which encouraged the on-going spiritual growth of each participant. What may have seemed to be a task-oriented activity was used to equip and teach skills that group members use to this day.

Measurable versus Intangible Results

The time Barnabas and Saul spent together in their mutual ministry in Antioch reaped several tangible and intangible benefits. Although they served together only for a short period, the fruit of their ministry had eternal results.

Acts 11:25 speaks of the great numbers of people who were taught, indicating fruitful ministry. This would be characteristic of the ministry that the two would later experience on their missionary journey. When these two Spirit-filled men taught and preached, people responded to the message and came into a new relationship with God through Jesus, and the Church grew in its numbers.

These converts also grew in their newfound faith towards maturity. This growth was not only noted by those within the Church, but also by those on the outside. Acts 11:26 records that the disciples were first called "Christians" at Antioch. This was a term which was meant to be derogatory, literally meaning "little Christs." The believers were seen as examples of Jesus, or as people who displayed the characteristics and qualities of their true Leader. This shows that a tangible result of Barnabas and Saul's ministry was the maturing of the believers.

Antioch also became a place of multiplied ministries. The prophecy of Agabus, predicting a famine that would encompass the world, was quickly responded to by the actions of the believers. Not only were the people of the church open and willing to hear what God had to say, but they were willing to respond to the revealed need. This does not appear to be a result of the coaxing of Barnabas or Saul, but rather reflects an attitude of ministry that prevailed in the congregation.

All of these tangible benefits were a result of the time the two leaders spent in ministry together. There were, however, many other intangible benefits that are not necessarily recognized at first glance.

One of the results of their time together was the full extent of the influence of Barnabas' character and integrity upon Saul's life. There is no way to measure the attitude changes or transformations which took place. One cannot spend time together with a man or woman of God and not learn from their prayer habits, devotional practices, and sense of integrity. While there is no way to measure the extent of the influence of Barnabas upon Saul, it quite obviously took place and reaped a great harvest.

Another intangible result of the time Barnabas and Saul spent together was the ever-increasing credibility in life and ministry of Saul. Before the year spent together with Barnabas, we see a secretive, perhaps unsure Saul. He had spent the better part of the last seventeen years in Damascus, Arabia, and Tarsus. Church history gives us no clear explanation for the long period of silence between his departure for Tarsus in Acts 9:30 and his year spent together with Barnabas in Acts 11:25-30. That Saul emerged as a different person after his time with Barnabas is undeniable.

Finally, the members of the Antioch church witnessed the start of missionary stirrings in their hearts and minds. Rather than being concerned with their own state of affairs, they thought of the needs of their sister church in Jerusalem. A short time later we see this same church responding to the Holy Spirit and the beginnings of a true missionary movement. This local church followed the example of its leaders and was obedient to the Great Commission. It became the base for evangelism and discipleship that launched out to the known world.

Could any of the results that are related here have happened without Barnabas and Saul spending years ministering together? There is no way to second-guess God, but probably things would not have been the same. The relational ministry Barnabas initiated with Saul accomplished more than the edification of the young church in Antioch. It was an example of God's perfect, *kairos* timing in the lives of these two men.[2]

The Greek word *kairos* is used in the New Testament to refer to God's sovereignty in the events of human history. This is different from *chronos* time, which refers to a chronological ordering of events. In Galatians 4:4-5, Paul used the word *kairos* to describe God's sense of perfect timing, stating that "when the set time had fully come, God sent his Son, born of a woman, born under the law, to redeem those under the law, that we might receive adoption to sonship." God's *kairos* timing occurs when He brings people and circumstances together at a specific time to accomplish His purposes.

God has not changed the way He works in our lives. He orchestrates special relationships that flourish and result in changed lives. Often, just at the right time, He brings a younger and less experienced person into the life of an older, seasoned mentor. The result, much as in the case of Barnabas and Saul, is an example of God's *kairos* timing which produces eternal fruit.

There is no substitute for time spent together in a mentoring relationship. It helps to develop and deepen our relationships and teamwork. It is not a question of quantity time versus the quality of time spent together, as the sharing of one's life is not something done over a few brief and shallow encounters. While there is no magical formula as to how much time is needed, the undeniable truth is that time spent together is an important element in seeing a relationship germinate and produce lasting fruit.

Proverbs 27:17 states this principle in other words:
"As iron sharpens iron, so one person sharpens another."

It would seem Barnabas recognized this need in his own life. He would have never gone to Tarsus if he didn't think this way.

The miracle of the story at the beginning of this chapter is that after spending time together with Tim swinging hammers, I agreed to take on a small part of the dramatic presentation. I also became a member of the youth choir. While I never did develop in the area of music—something my wife can attest to—I thoroughly enjoyed the dramatic presentation. In fact, the use of drama is one of my most effective tools for youth.

Tim never confessed that his first phone call had mixed motives, but I believe his true intention had nothing to do with my participation in the youth choir or with getting a stage built. What we did together was not his main concern: he wanted to initiate a friendship and develop a relationship.

Looking back I thank God for Tim's willingness to spend time with me, even if it was doing something as ordinary as swinging a hammer on a couple of Saturday afternoons. I thank God for the "Barnabas" who came into my life, first and foremost as my friend, but also as one who would point me to Christ. If only Tim had known what he was getting himself into. Who knows? Maybe he did.

Study Guide

ACTIVE LEARNING ...

In groups of two or three, answer the following questions and then share your work with the larger group.

1. What are the three most important lessons or principles a mentor can pass along to a disciple?

2. Make a list of two or three activities that could be used to teach each of the three principles identified in the first question. (Example: Faith can be taught by rappelling down a fifty-foot cliff, as well as by keeping a journal in a prayer partnership.)

3. How can the activities in question 2 serve to deepen relationships? What is the importance of active learning in the mentoring process?

CONSIDER ...

Read the passages listed below, carefully answering the questions that follow.

1. In John 1:43-51, Jesus called His disciples according to their personalities and characteristics. How does the calling of Nathanael reflect this truth? What are the personal factors that Jesus touched upon to impact Nathanael's life?
2. In John 13:1-17, Jesus taught His disciples through His personal example. What was the principal lesson Jesus sought to teach in this passage? List two or three modern applications we could use to impart this same lesson.

3. In Acts 9:26-30 and 11:22-26, what lessons did Saul learn from the personal example of Barnabas in these first two recorded encounters? How did their time spent together serve to deepen their partnership?

RESPOND ...

Principle: There is no replacement for time spent with godly men or women. As you rub shoulders with them, something rubs off on you.

1. Identify one person who has impacted your life as a result of spending time together. What did you do with them? What did you learn from them?

2. In what way does the above principle apply to the life of Barnabas? Why are relationships vitally important in passing along godly character?

Make a list of two or three activities you could do with a person you consider to be a disciple. Make a commitment to God (and to your study group) to do one of the activities during the upcoming week.

CHAPTER 4
TIDDLYWINKS IS NOT A TEAM SPORT

It was a rainy Saturday afternoon and I was at home with my two young children, waiting for my wife, Rhonda, to return from a worship practice. My kids were bored and looking for something to do. In a brief moment of creativity I thought of a game we could play.

The game itself wasn't new, but it was to my kids. They cheered with glee as I announced we were going to play tiddlywinks.

We didn't have the game, so we improvised with small cardboard disks called pogs. Using a larger disk called a slammer, we applied pressure and flipped the disks towards a plastic bowl placed in the middle of the room. Each disk that landed in the dish was worth one point. Soon the air was filled with mini-flying saucers and my kid's laughter. That's when another problem surfaced.

"You're on my team," announced Brett, my five-year-old son, speaking directly to me.

"No," retorted Kayla, my seven-year-old daughter. "Dad's always on my team!"

"But Mom's not here, so Dad's on my team!"

"It doesn't matter! He's always on my team!"

"Hold it, hold it!" I interjected. "I'll play on both teams."

That didn't go over very well and another argument erupted as the two discussed whether the rules allowed for a person to play on both teams.

Finally, I announced, "Tiddlywinks is not a team sport! Either we play every person for himself, or we don't play at all."

A little surprised, both Kayla and Brett looked at me and said, "In our family we always play on teams."

I wondered whether our hard work to instill an attitude of cooperation and teamwork had been shot in an instant. Kayla and Brett now considered the concept of the "every man for himself" approach, something we had preached against. But at the end of the game, both said they would rather play on teams, either sharing the joys of winning or the sorrows of losing with another person.

———

One of the great lessons we learn from the life of Barnabas is his ability to instill in his disciples an attitude of teamwork. Barnabas not only made this a priority, but working in teams was his *modus operandi* and a key part of his leadership style. He did so for a number of reasons, and his example is worth noting. This chapter will show that, unlike tiddlywinks, ministry is very much a team activity.

Formation of a Ministry Team

The account of Acts 11:22-26 gives a picture of the process Barnabas followed in the formation of his ministry relationship with Saul. The observations made from Barnabas' example of ministry in Antioch set a wonderful model for the formation of ministry teams. His pattern also follows the principles Jesus instilled in his disciples. This model was also followed by Paul and others in the New Testament.

When Barnabas was sent by the Jerusalem church, he first took on the role of an observer. We do not know how much time he did this for, but his first task was to watch the church in action. Only later was he involved in a fruitful ministry of teaching and encouragement. Somewhere in this process he observed needs that were not being met and he sought out others to participate with him.

Barnabas took the initiative to seek out Saul and to invite him to be one of the members of his ministry team. Having identified the needs which his personal ministry addressed, Barnabas sought someone who would complement his ministry. In other words, Barnabas was pro-active in the formation of a team which would add to the overall ministry of the Church.

We are not always given the opportunity to choose the formation of our ministry team or whom we will disciple. However, when afforded this opportunity, we need to make the most of it. This is done by prayerfully seeking those with a gift-mix different from ours, or by being deliberate in identifying the areas in which we can minister to those who will be our disciples. The ability to choose our team members does not guarantee a successful, functioning group, but it is desirable when compared to ministry situations or teams that are never thought out or deliberately formed.

When we are not the one to choose our team members, or when God brings individuals into our lives to disciple, we need to rely on God's sovereignty, leading, and wisdom. There are times when God will bring a person into our life as a deliberate part of His plan to teach us a lesson, or vice versa. As God leads, there are times when an imposed team structure results in a positive mix of spiritual gifts and personalities who work well together.

There were also character qualities Barnabas sought in those he would include in his ministry team. Something from his previous meeting with Saul in Jerusalem captured his attention and led Barnabas to go to Tarsus to seek him out. These characteristics included elements of common interest, but also included elements of differences in their personalities and giftedness.

What both men had in common is important in understanding why they worked well together. Both men were Hellenistic Jews from the tribe of Levi. They understood and lived within a context similar to that of Antioch. More important, they were both committed to the growth of the church, both numerically and in terms of spiritual maturity. This mutual foundation was important in understanding one another and working together.

What both men did not share in common is equally important in understanding why they worked well together. Barnabas sought out someone with different, yet complementary spiritual gifts. Barnabas was a consoling, pastoral leader while Saul was an apostle with a drive to preach the Gospel to the unreached. Barnabas was a disciple-maker and teacher, while Saul had a focus on evangelism and apologetics in his ministry. Each man's giftedness complemented the other. Their diversity multiplied their ministry effectiveness and did not lead to division.

Barnabas and Saul are a good example of unity in the midst of diversity. Their ability to form a team in spite of their different personalities was the key to the success of their relationship. Their shared commitment to Christ-like character, combined with unique spiritual giftedness, made Barnabas and Saul a dynamic duo used by God. [1]

Finally, Barnabas was able to form the Antioch ministry team around an objective that was task-oriented without being program-bound. Barnabas' invitation to Saul was to accompany him to teach and encourage the believers in Antioch. This ministry task offered Saul the opportunity to learn through active involvement in ministry. Neither the structure that was developed nor the methodology they used became the focus of their ministry.

Barnabas and Saul developed a pattern of ministering within the Church. Each took on specific tasks or duties. We do not know what their ministry looked like in terms of programmed activities, but we do know that when the Holy Spirit called them to change these responsibilities in Acts 13:3, they were open to this change. This was aided by the fact that other capable leaders were also trained. They did not see themselves as the key to maintaining or keeping the ministry going in Antioch. Although they had developed their methods and had some form of structure in the local church, they were not bound by them.

In my experience, personal mentoring works best when it includes training and participation in specific ministry tasks. This can take on many forms, from leadership groups to evangelistic drama teams. The goal is to include our disciples in real ministry situations. This shows a commitment to active learning, and teaches practical skills that equip our disciples for ministry.

However, there needs to be an openness to change structures according to the situation or individuals with whom you are working. What worked in one place or with one individual does not necessarily "click" with another. Methodologies and structures are not sacred. What matters in the mentoring process is that our learners are equipped and actively involved in ministry. They need to get a taste of the ways God can use them. The wise mentor learns that there is a fine line between being effective in programs or ministries, and being bound by them.

The three aspects considered from the formation of the Antioch ministry team are equally important to the formation of ministry teams in local churches. When given the opportunity, a team can be chosen in a deliberate and pro-active manner. It can address the real needs in a church or ministry. Equally important, the selection of team members should be based on spiritual gifts that complement one another. This leads to increased effectiveness and multiplied ministries. Finally, it is important to recognize that the methods and structures we use are tools to accomplish ministry in a given context. They are not its reason for existence.

Benefits of Team Ministry Approach

Many benefits flowed from the merging of Barnabas and Saul into a ministry team. These benefits affected their personal growth as well as that of their church.

One of the immediate benefits of a team ministry approach is multiplied effectiveness. Barnabas had a purpose in seeking out a person whose gifts and personality were different from his own. This had a multiplying effect upon the number of people reached through the Antioch church. Those Barnabas would touch with his personal shepherding ministry style were different from those the evangelist Saul could reach. Together their individual ministries would be multiplied, not limited.

Barnabas did not go to Antioch as a "one-man show" or with a "head honcho" attitude. He didn't take over and bulldoze his plans and vision. He was committed to working with others on a team.

Only Jesus is able to minister to every person and every need. We are finite beings with limitations. This applies to our spiritual gifts as well as to our natural abilities. God's design for the Church is for individuals to come together in community to express His grace and to minister to the needs of people. In doing so, there is a fullness to the ministry accomplished.

The wise leader is able to recognize his or her shortcomings and to seek others to fill in the gaps where they are not gifted or talented. These leaders are able to do so in such a way that they build into the lives of those who make up a part of their ministry team, helping them along in their spiritual growth.

A second benefit in team ministry is the provision for times of mutual encouragement and prayer. This differs greatly from a "Lone Ranger" approach that does not see the need for the involvement of others. Having someone alongside to answer to, pray with, and lift us up in times of discouragement, fine-tunes us and makes us more effective in our ministries. It also leads to healthier ministries that have a broader and farther-reaching impact.

The year of Barnabas and Saul's ministry in Antioch included times of mutual support and encouragement. An integral part of the relationship of the Antioch ministry team included significant times in prayer (Acts 13:1-3). This follows the pattern Barnabas observed in the early Church (Acts 1:14; 2:1, 42). It included times of intercession for their needs and to seek God's will and vision for their ministries. It was coupled with times of fasting and prayer. Together these leaders exercised various spiritual disciplines, which not only served to increase their effectiveness in ministry, but also deepened their relationship.

I am thankful for the times of prayer I have experienced with colleagues in ministry team situations. I have been built up, encouraged, and helped to focus on God's perspective in situations. While group prayer times do not replace our personal devotional times with God, they serve to encourage a greater interdependence and sense of partnership in ministry.

The element of accountability is another benefit of ministry teams. When we work with a team, we know we will need to give a report to a group of people, motivating us to put action to our words. This does not have to be a threatening exercise, especially when done in an atmosphere of mutual support, vision, and participation.

This principle is seen in the lives of Barnabas and Saul in Acts 14:27 when they hold the inaugural missions conference. The first thing they did when they came back to their sending church was to give a full report of all God did in them and through them. Their sense of responsibility to those who sent them and supported them is commendable.

Accountability to others is a biblical principle that builds character. It makes us better leaders and sharpens our skills. While some see giving account for their actions as a threatening situation, a positive way of seeing accountability is "the enlisting of others to help you keep the promises you have made to God."[2] This viewpoint affirms the fact that we need others to help us become the people God wants us to be.

The exact configuration of an accountability structure varies with each situation. At times it can be carried out in a group setting, while in other instances it is best done between two individuals. In all situations there is a need for transparency and trust between the people involved. The principal function is to encourage rather than being confrontational. In a team setting, accountability involves regular meetings.

The Church has suffered when leaders have not followed the principle of accountability in a ministry team approach. Many of the scandals and abuses of power that have rocked the Church can be traced to individuals who acted on their own and did not seek others to help them in their areas of temptation. Prudent and wise leaders welcome accountability structures, as they not only protect their ministry and reputation, but also those of the Church.

Finally, a team approach to ministry provides for the training of future leadership. This is especially the case in structures that call for apprentices or co-leaders. The commitment to train other leaders makes continuity of ministry a priority and not something which depends on one particular person.

Saul was not the only future leader trained by Barnabas. Acts 13 speaks of a number of capable leaders present in the Church. While Saul stands out as the rising star among those leaders, he was not alone. Barnabas may have been thinking Saul would take his place as the pastor of the church, but others had also been prepared. When the time came for the two to respond to the leading of the Holy Spirit, there was no leadership void.

I had the pleasure of participating on a church board that not only gave lip service to the principle of constantly training new leaders, but put it into practice. The ministries of the local church were divided into three key areas: pastoral care, evangelism, and administration. Each division had one person in charge of a team. An older, experienced leader was coupled with younger men or women who showed potential in the specific area of ministry. This approach guaranteed the continuation of ministry within the structure this church adopted, and decreased the shock when there was a leadership change.

I am thankful that for many years I have worked under an organization committed to a philosophy of team ministry. It has increased and multiplied my effectiveness. I have personally benefited from times of encouragement and prayer. I have also been blessed by having people to whom I knew I would be accountable for my use of time, resources, and money. Others could be trained in this less threatening model, because all of the responsibilities were not thrown upon one person. These factors of mutual ministry have enriched my experience and multiplied my effectiveness.

How to Effectively Kill a Team Ministry: Three Dangers to Avoid

What makes the difference between an effective and functional ministry team over a struggling and ineffective team? I'd like to suggest three very important "make-it or break-it" areas that will help a team to thrive—or effectively kill any hope of lasting ministry. Three dangers must be avoided at all cost, as they affect the relationship of the ministry team, as well as its effectiveness in touching people's lives.

First, we have to recognize that lack of effective communication leads to sure failure. There needs to be a strong commitment on the part of leaders and all participants to make it work. There is a need for clear and effective lines of authority within the group. There is a need for openness and an opportunity for all to express themselves. Prayer must play an important role as the team tackles tough or thorny issues. All of this takes effort, commitment, and planning. Without clear communication, a team is destined to flounder.

The structure a ministry team adopts to facilitate communication may take various forms. Weekly meetings for prayer, encouragement and planning are used by some groups. Meeting times may be less frequent in some situations, but they are necessary to focus on working together to achieve the purposes set forth by the group.

I participated on a ministry team that divided its meetings into three key activities. Twice a month we met to pray and plan, discussing the ministry needs we faced in our individual areas. One meeting per month was dedicated to prayer, both for ministry and individual needs. One other meeting was set aside for the training of relevant ministry skills, focusing on the aspect of learning together. Another goal was to eat one meal per month as a team, providing less formal times to be together. All of this served to develop a sense of partnership and unity.

Another reason for ineffective team ministries rests on the fact that some leadership styles reflect rugged individualism. Strong leaders are seen as those who do not depend upon others, but who forge ahead on their own. Their abilities to make decisions, take action, and accomplish great feats for the Kingdom of God are encouraged and even applauded.

This sense of individualism has become popular in some circles. Paul is referred to as one who knew what he wanted to do—preach the Gospel where it had not yet been preached—and went out and did it. Little or no thought is given to his commitment to take others with him, nor the years he spent in training with Barnabas. He is applauded as a visionary and his accomplishments are given as a justification for acting outside of accountability structures. While this goes against biblical teaching and is contrary to Paul's writings, it is no doubt prevalent in many branches of evangelical thinking. This model can take on the form of a spiritual dictatorship and presents many inherent dangers.

A visionary does not have to be a person who refuses to listen to others or work with them. A true leader enlists the help of others to accomplish the calling God places on his or her life. Accountability structures are needed to fine-tune and weed out anything which is not an integral part of God's purpose for that person. The focus does not have to be on personality or results, but on training others to ensure an ongoing ministry that glorifies God. Such leaders recognize that effective leadership is not guaranteed by a strong hand, as often the followers of a dictatorial leader are like clones who cannot think or act for themselves.

Finally, a sense of competitiveness can crush a team's effectiveness and squash the spirit of some. This is a hard lesson to learn as society conditions us to compete with others in nearly every other area of life.

The "bigger is better" attitude which prevails in our culture is an accomplice to a competitive spirit. Many come into a ministry situation with this attitude, comparing themselves to the church down the road, or to a teammate. This can have destructive results upon a person as they lose focus and begin to work out of a sense of duty. It can also lead to a downward spiral that discourages and leaves its victims rendered useless.

Working in God's Kingdom is not a grand competition with an impressive mansion as the prize for those who win the most souls or have the largest church. Paul comments in Philippians 3:10 that the goal or prize is to know Christ, not to stand out as a superstar who deserves acclamation.[3] It's not a contest!

The dangers of competitiveness among team members are not ignored by a wise leader. Rather, a leader needs to work to establish a keen sense of teamwork. Often this involves laying aside the right to personal recognition and acclaim. One who can applaud the accomplishments of other team members has learned to master the principles displayed in the life of Barnabas. The true measure of a leader is the ability to facilitate the success of others. He or she helps others to identify God's calling in their lives, and to become the person God wants them to be.

———

One final point is worth noting. The development of ministry teams is not unique to Barnabas or Saul. It follows the pattern Jesus set for His disciples. Jesus sought others to participate together with Him in his ministry. He formed a group of disciples who would carry on the ministry He initiated. He sent them out in groups of at least two, to assure that they would have mutual support and encouragement in the midst of opposition (Luke 10:1). The disciples later formed an organizational structure that required accountability from those who had gone out to preach the Gospel to the four corners of the world. First and foremost, the team-ministry approach is something initiated by Jesus.

Unlike tiddlywinks, ministry is indeed a team venture. Wise leaders teach the value of teamwork through their example and commitment to help others develop gifts and skills. They affirm the principles learned from the example of Barnabas and the first ministry team in Antioch, which did not see the inclusion of others as a threat or hindrance. Rather, they multiplied their ministry effectiveness by training and working alongside others.

Study Guide

ACTIVE LEARNING ...

In a group of two or three, make a list of five individuals who would make up your "dream team" for a large church ministry situation. Choose from biblical characters, historical figures, or current leaders. Answer the following questions once you have established the five leaders and their positions on your all-star squad. Be prepared to share your work with the larger group (if applicable).

1. Who is the captain of your "dream team"? Why was this person chosen to be leader?

2. What role would each of the other team members fill? What is the purpose behind each selection?

3. What would you do to ensure that these individuals would work together as a team? Is it realistic to think a team of all-stars can have an effective ministry?

CONSIDER ...

Read the passages listed below, carefully answering the questions that follow.

1. In Luke 10:1-16, what instructions did Jesus give to His disciples? What are the principles relevant to team ministry in this passage?

2. In 1 Peter 4:7-11, which aspects of this list of spiritual gifts speak of mutual or co-dependent ministry? What central truth did Peter seek to communicate?

3. In 1 Corinthians 1:10-17, what does Paul state about his main role in the growth process of the believers in Corinth? What is the role of the other leaders mentioned? What do we learn about Paul's attitude towards teamwork and mutual ministry?

RESPOND ...

Principle: The mentor/disciple relationship affirms interdependence and diversity of spiritual gifts.

1. Make a list of three people who work together as a team (either a ministerial or secular group). What task do they seek to accomplish? What are the benefits reaped by a teamwork approach? What is the secret to their success or failure?

2. Consider a group of people with whom you work. Evaluate your commitment to clear communication, a teamwork approach, and eliminating competition. What can be done to improve in each of the three areas mentioned?

What are you doing to include others in your personal ministry? Identify one or two people you can include in a future event or study group. Pray for opportunities to impart principles of teamwork to these people.

CHAPTER 5
DIARY OF A DISCIPLE-MAKER

What have I got myself into? I shook my head as I surveyed the group assembled for a follow-up meeting about a recent spiritual retreat. *Lord, what do you want me to do with this group?"*

Seven people stared back at me. They longed to hear words of encouragement and direction for their lives. A tired salesman sat at the other end of the table, his weary wife at his side. An older lady sat to one side, her face lined with painful memories from a bitter family situation. Several students sat on the other side, arms crossed. I knew they struggled with interpersonal relationships. One was a young Christian and unsure of the depth of his commitment to God. Four of the seven were at the point of throwing in the towel and leaving their local church.

This was the group God had given me to disciple and teach. I could only wonder what God might do through them. If it wasn't for the "Driftwood Principle"—seeing people for who they can become and not only for who they are—I might have dismissed the class early and headed home.[1]

All members of the group were like uncut diamonds, each one with rough or jagged edges but God was at work in their lives. As they sat before me, their attitude of *teachability* encouraged me to proceed with the class.

If we could read the diary of Barnabas we would probably be astounded at its content. It would be interesting to compare his descriptions of Saul from their first meeting, over their year in ministry, and to the point where Saul went out on his own.

Perhaps Barnabas would share his frustrations and challenges as he dealt with someone who had a different personality. His journal would probably include some discouraging entries. It would be enlightening to read the accounts of when things began to click and his disciple began to take steps and then leaps towards maturity. All of this would lead to a deeper understanding of the journey Barnabas and Saul took as they developed their ministry relationship. It would reveal a skillful mentor used by God to make an impact on the world as he influenced individuals.

The diary of Barnabas would also reveal a man of godly character who exemplified the specific characteristics he wanted to build into the life of his disciple. Barnabas recognized potential in the life of his disciple, emulated Christ-like character, and helped Saul discover God's will and purpose for his life. These skills, which are essential elements in the mentor's toolbox, were first lived out and then taught to his followers.

F.A.T. Disciples

We live in a world of acronyms. Just ask anyone what UN, or AIDS, or FBI stand for? While they may not always get all the words of the acronym right, they are more than likely able to identify its general meaning. One small word explains a whole phrase and carries connotations that are understood by all.

The acronym *FAT* is a good description of the character qualities that need to be built into a disciple of Christ. The disciple needs to be faithful, available, and teachable.[2] While this acronym may not be politically correct, it does describe the life of a person who will grow and flourish under the influence of a godly mentor.

Faithful

One of the qualities that stands out in the life of Barnabas is his faithfulness. He was entrusted with the task of surveying the situation of the newly formed group of believers in Antioch. He would later be given the responsibility of being the leader of the missionary troop that left for Cyprus and Asia Minor. He was a respected and trustworthy witness at the Jerusalem Council. Barnabas, the one who came alongside those who needed a helping hand, was a man of confidence.

Barnabas faithfully committed himself to a person and did not look back. He stuck his neck on the proverbial chopping block when he brought Saul to the leaders of the Jerusalem church. His reputation was on the line, not Saul's. Barnabas would take his commitment one step further, inviting

Saul to join the ministry team in Antioch. Saul must have flashed a broad smile on the day Barnabas knocked at his door, realizing that Barnabas' first act of believing in him was backed up an opportunity to join the ministry team in Antioch. Barnabas' faithful reinforcement of his belief in Saul's potential was inspiring.

Years later, Barnabas demonstrated faithfulness and commitment to Mark, even though he proved to be unfaithful on the first missionary journey. This act was the first step towards a complete restoration of Mark, who would later pen the Gospel that bears his name.

"I believe in you" and "I'm committed to your growth" are among the most edifying phrases a mentor can say to those under his or her care. This is especially true when such words are backed up by action, which speaks louder than words. It is unlikely for a disciple to develop faithfulness and dedication in their life without their mentor's verbal affirmations and corresponding deeds.

Faithfulness is first modeled then built into the life of a disciple in three specific areas. A personal relationship with God is the first aspect to be fleshed out. It is exemplified in a life of devotion and commitment to personal and spiritual growth. Secondly, faithfulness needs to go beyond the personal level to the corporate level, shown in dedication to the community of believers of the person's local church. Third, a mentoring relationship requires a commitment to meet, pray, and learn together. These three elements, irreplaceable in the development of a true follower of Christ, need to first be observed in a leader, then taught to those God brings into their life.

New Christians do not necessarily come in ready-made packages, nor do they display deep maturity and commitment from the beginning of their walk with God. It is imperative that the person charged with their care gives them bite-sized challenges that will require an ever- deepening dedication in the areas mentioned above. Their loyalty to God, His work, and His people, should grow with time. The wise mentor knows that the goal of mentorship is to deepen their disciple's commitment and daily walk with the Lord.

Available

Barnabas was open and available to the leading of God. When it came time for him to leave Jerusalem and go to Antioch, he went. When the Holy Spirit called Barnabas and Saul to go where the Gospel had not been preached, they got on board the ship. When the two leaders disagreed over the inclusion of Mark, Barnabas was willing to take on a new disciple and continue the work he believed God called him to accomplish.

Likewise, Saul showed no hesitation in accompanying Barnabas when he received the invitation to help out in Antioch. Chapters 13 and 14 of the book of Acts show the way the men took advantage of each opportunity, accepting it as God's leading. Later in life, Paul would encourage the Colossian believers to "make the most of every opportunity" (Col. 4:5).

Availability is an attitude. It is something that can be held back. It is not a blind "yes" to everything that comes along, but it is a willingness to consider, to try, and to depart from one's own comfortable ways. This coming out of one's own comfort zone is the expression of obedience God desires to see in each of His followers.

Availability is another key element which needs to be modeled in a mentoring relationship. Those whom we seek to reach need to know we make our time with them a priority in our lives. While the issue of "quality time" is real, there is no substitute for the quantity of time it takes to develop deep relationships with people.

As an older teenager, I participated in a leadership training group that met every second Monday evening for a pre-established period of eight months. Instead of being a study group, our time was set aside to learn life and ministry skills to become leaders at a Christian camp. The initial group was composed of nearly a dozen teens. All of us agreed to faithfully participate, a commitment we kept for the first weeks. However, by the end of the year there were only five who remained.

Many of the "drop outs" of the group did not leave because of a lack of desire to participate. Rather, they had taken on more than they could fulfill. Their other commitments took priority and the promise to participate soon became impossible to complete.

I was once approached by a young man who told me he would like to spend time together to pray and talk about our relationships with the Lord. I welcomed his interest, seeing his pro-activeness as a good beginning to a mentorship situation. Immediately we set to the task of working out a meeting time. That's when we ran into some problems.

The young man's family owned and operated a thriving business which required a great deal of his time and attention. He was on call twenty-four hours a day, and needed to respond to emergencies that took him to all corners of the country. He said he was not in control of his time and could rarely meet. In the end our relationship did not develop, nor did any real mentorship take place.

Other people don't want to develop deep relationships. They may have all of the latest gadgets and novelties that technology can afford them, but missing meetings or a lack of availability shows that discipleship is not a priority in their lives. Some people hide behind busyness, seeing any deep relationship as a threat. Often these people reveal their insecurity by a lack of willingness to change areas of their lives. While a person might express a desire to work together or to develop a mentoring relationship, their true priorities are indicated by their unwillingness to set aside time for meeting together.

Teachable

The final character quality to look for in a future leader is *teachablity*. This is a characteristic which needs to be seen in both the mentor and their disciples. If the leader of a mentoring relationship isn't committed to lifelong learning, he cannot expect his disciples to get beyond a dull edge.

Barnabas and Saul were constant learners. The events of the first missionary journey are a list of the experiences and challenges Barnabas and Saul were forced to face (Acts 13 and 14). Saul expressed his ongoing apprenticeship in the things of God, stating, "Not that I have already obtained all this, or have already arrived at my goal, but... I press on toward the goal to win the prize for which God has called me heavenward in Christ Jesus" (Philippians 3:12, 14). This attitude of lifelong learning not only displayed true humility, but also reflected an attitude of dependence upon God to be their teacher.

As with the case of faithfulness and availability, a teachable spirit is something that is caught more than taught.

One pastor told me of his struggle to encourage his church members to get to Bible classes and to participate actively in their own education. He stopped in his tracks, however, when I asked him when he had last taken a class. Instead of giving an answer, he began to list his excuses. Lack of time, finances, and overload of responsibilities at work and home were all a part of his reasons for not personally pursuing further studies. With as much tact and love as I could manage, I told him, "Your people will only begin to plug into the learning opportunities that are offered once they see your love for learning. You need to lead by example."

The next week he registered for a class in our leadership training institute. As he began to share with his congregation the many things he was learning through his classes, things began to change in his church. Only a few months later he saw a completely different attitude among his church members.

A person who does not have a teachable spirit will show some clear signs of this attitude. "I already know that," and "That's nothing new" are two phrases repeated by a person who does not want to learn. Some express their lack of interest in a subject by their lateness, while others use physical gestures such as a posture of disinterest or over-exaggerated yawning. Others expose their unteachable spirit by fidgeting and not keeping still long enough to finish or complete a task. They ask irrelevant questions or interrupt your conversations with hypothetical interjections.

Surprisingly, the two types of leaders on opposite ends of the ministry experience spectrum tend to be the least teachable. The new graduate or person recently placed into a leadership role, as well as the person who has been in ministry for many years can be among the least flexible and teachable people. It takes great wisdom and tact to encourage these two types of people to see that their attitude towards learning affects their spiritual growth, as well as that of those to whom they are ministering. For this reason it is all the more important that a person who takes on a discipleship role be a lifelong learner.

Rick Warren, author of *The Purpose Driven Church,* correctly identifies this characteristic when he states, "All leaders are learners. The moment you stop learning, you stop leading."[3]

Faithfulness, availability, and teachability are not taught in a series of lessons. They are qualities that are imparted by example. They are nurtured by focusing on the aspect of character development in the mentoring process, not just on the material taught, nor on the method used.

Seeing and Unleashing God's Potential in your Disciples

Barnabas displayed another ability that greatly affected his ministry. He was able to overcome the distrust of Saul that bound the leaders in Jerusalem, and also the failures of Mark. Somehow he saw beyond who they were to who they could become if they were given the opportunity to prove themselves.

The ability to see potential in the lives of the people who are younger followers of Christ is a great tool in the hands of a skilled mentor. While there is an aspect of spiritual discernment that certainly can help one to see latent talents and gifts, the following list gives some practical ways a mentor can look at those God has given them to disciple.

1. Include teaching on the spiritual gifts early in the mentorin process, especially as it relates to the ministerial gifts listed in Romans 12:6-8.[4] New Christians need to be taught that God imparts each believer with at least one spiritual gift. This gift is to be used for the edification of the church. Teaching about the spiritual gifts and their biblical guidelines will help a young Christian to discover the person God made them to be.

Allow participants to identify the areas that appeal to them, paying special attention to those they would like to develop over the course of your time together. This needs to be reevaluated along the way, based on the experiences a disciple faces as he or she takes their first steps in reaching out to others. Careful observations of personality traits and natural abilities can help disciples as they verbalize and seek direction to know and use their gifts for the glory of God.

2. Listen to your disciples as they share their dreams and communicate the specific leading of God upon their lives. Make special note of the changes they express in their purpose for living, observing the transformation of heart that a deepening relationship with the Lord has precipitated. Their aspirations often reveal a seed God has planted.

Carlinhos, a young Brazilian Christian once shared his dream to be a disc jockey. He wanted to begin a radio ministry that would radically challenge teens and young adults in their walk with the Lord. Some of his ideas seemed wild and far-fetched to me, but we prayed together and committed his dream to God. I am glad I listened to Carlinhos and did not say what first came to my mind, as for many years he hosted a weekly broadcast that reached hundreds of young people. He passed away as a young man, but his dream became a reality and he left his mark.

3. Expose learners to a variety of experiences and ministry situations. There are many practical ways this can be done. Take a seminar on evangelism and watch as your disciples make their first attempts at sharing their faith. Teach a class together and make special note of their abilities and sense of accomplishment as they tackle this task. Attending a missions conference may be the spark that ignites a heart set on fire for the nations. Include a broad variety of ministry situations. You never know which experience will initiate a lifelong ministry in the lives of those you are mentoring.

4. Observe your disciples as they take their first steps to minister to others. What are the areas of ministry in which they seem to thrive? Do they look forward to involvement in teaching, evangelism, or helping others? Encourage them to be faithful stewards of their gifts and abilities. Develop these gifts in practical ways. Your comments, based on observations made while they minister, can spur them on to fruitful service for God.

5. Pray for patience, discernment, and wisdom as you seek to encourage those you are helping. New Christians often lack God's perspective on circumstances in their lives and need someone who will not get bogged down with or be bothered by their difficult times. Ask God to help you perceive them through His eyes, that you will see who they might become. In doing this you are affirming God's sovereignty in your life, as well in their lives, acknowledging that He has brought you together with His purposes in mind.

As I began my class that evening I needed to ask God to allow me to see my students through His eyes. Instead of seeing a tired salesman, I needed to consider that man's strong desire to start a new church. His wife had recently expressed her dream to become an author of children's books. The elderly lady wanted to study to be a counselor, helping others face difficult circumstances. Some of those ready to pack their bags and give up on their local church were called to be missionaries. Each one had great potential when seen through the eyes of God.

As I further surveyed the group I realized that each person was proving themselves to be faithful, available, and teachable. They had sacrificed their time and had made an effort to prepare for the class. They were eager to learn from each other as they shared the lessons God had taught them during the retreat. They showed desire to grow, to know more of God, and to apply His Word to their lives. I was privileged to be a part of God's eternal purposes in their lives. As we began our class I prayed and thanked God for each person present.

Study Guide

ACTIVE LEARNING ...

1. Divide into small groups. On a large sheet of paper or poster board draw and design a "F.A.T.-o-Meter." This scale should measure the *faithfulness, availability,* and *teachability* of a disciple. For each character quality offer four or five levels of development.

    (Example: In a classroom setting faithfulness can be measured by:
    a. Showing up at meetings.
    b. Showing up at meetings on time.
    c. Preparing assignments for class., etc.

2. Present your "F.A.T.-o-Meter" to the larger group. Allow time for observations and questions.

CONSIDER ...

Do a F.A.T. test on the following biblical characters. Do they pass the test? Why or why not? What are the are the "make-it or break-it" aspects that help a person succeed?

1. King Saul (1 Samuel 9:1-2; 10:20-24; 15:13-35)

2. King David (1 Samuel 16:1-13, 2 Samuel 12:1-14, and Acts 13:21-22)

3. Peter (Matthew 14:22-33; John 13:31-38; and John 21:15-17)

4. Sinful Woman (Luke 7:36-50)

5. Rich Young Ruler (Mark 10:17-23)

6. Zacchaeus, the Tax Collector (Luke 19:1-9)

RESPOND ...

Principle: An effective mentor displays the qualities of faithfulness, availability, and *teachability* in their own lives. Only then can they hope to see the same characteristics displayed in the life of their disciples.

1. Do a "F.A.T.-o-Meter" test on yourself. What are your strengths? In which area do you see the greatest need for growth?

2. What are you actively doing to ensure you are growing in each of the three areas listed? Identify one specific activity you can focus on during the upcoming week that will spur you on to growth and maturity.

Spend time in prayer (preferably with another person) and commit the activity listed in question 2 to God. Plan a time of accountability with your prayer partner.

CHAPTER 6
WOULD SOMEONE ANSWER THE PHONE

A dimly lit stage reveals a young woman sitting down, twiddling her thumbs as she impatiently waits for something to happen. The red phone on the table in front of her is the focus of her attention.

The monotony of the initial moments of the scene is broken when a young man walks on stage. He notices the unoccupied phone and walks over to the table, reaching out to pick up the receiver.

"No, you can't," the woman says.

"Why not?"

"It's just that this phone is …well, it's busy!"

"Doesn't look to busy to me," the young man responds.

"Well, maybe not right now, but it will be. You'll see, I'm waiting for the call."

"You're waiting for *a* call?"

"Not a call, silly. I'm waiting for *the* call."

"I don't get what you're trying to …"

He stops as he realizes the full extent of what she has just told him. "You're expecting a call from…" He stops as he points upwards.

"Yes, I am. And I'm going to stay here until I get it!" She crosses her arms and flops back into her chair.

The Call, a missions-related sketch, tells the story of two people who are seeking God's will for their lives.[1] The ensuing dialogue between Dave and Cheryl in the next three scenes revolves around the question, what is *"the call?"*

Dave wants to phone his pastor to tell him of an acceptance letter to go to Bible College. Cheryl does not allow him to touch the phone because she is "waiting for the call." Dave, who leaves for his ministry preparation at the end of the first scene, returns in the second scene, only to find Cheryl in a deep sleep. She's still waiting for the call. The scenario repeats itself when Dave, who has supposedly been working as a youth pastor in the interval between the second and third scene, returns to find his friend locked in a holding pattern, unwilling to budge from her chair unless God miraculously calls her into action.

The hypothetical dialogue of the sketch is broken at the end of the third scene when the phone begins to ring. Cheryl, who can barely contain herself, retraces all of the steps of preparation that Dave took. She states that all of this has served for naught as she is now the one who is receiving *"the call."* Dave's desperate plea for Cheryl to answer the phone is the only thing that startles her out of her excited frenzy. Finally, she picks up the phone.

Cheryl's conversation with the other party is easy to follow. She explains her predicament and justifies her years of waiting for the call. However, disappointment is etched on her face as she glances over in Dave's direction. The last line of the play hushes the audience when Cheryl reluctantly hands Dave the phone. "It's for you!"

———————

There were no phones when Barnabas and Saul met with the leaders of the Antioch church for prayer and fasting. There was a primitive postal system, but there were no telegrams, no internet, no cell phones or email, and no means of modern telecommunication. Yet somehow God's message was received by the church and its leadership.

Barnabas and Saul's response to "the call" was the culmination of three phases God used to prepare them for this event. In each of these steps God blended people, circumstances, and His divine *kairos* timing to accomplish His purposes.[2] There was a phase in which a yearning to preach the Gospel in other cities was planted in their hearts. This was followed by a phase in which this idea grew and matured. This all led to a third phase of action and harvest. In Acts 13:1-3 Barnabas and Saul responded to God's direction and were sent out by the Antioch church to accomplish their mission. Their obedience resulted in the first true missionary movement.

The phases of God's will and call upon a person's life are important lessons to teach a disciple. They help us to recognize and take steps to complete God's purposes in the lives of people we disciple. As we help them to learn to listen to God's voice and to know His will, we can have a far-reaching impact for His Kingdom.

Phase I: God's Call is Planted in the Hearts of His Followers

God had planted the seeds of a missionary calling many years prior to the events of Acts 13. The presence of Barnabas on foreign soil, now pastor of the church in Antioch, is a testimony to this fact. Saul, right from the first moments of his conversion, is identified as a chosen vessel who would take the Gospel to the Gentiles. Both Barnabas and Saul had a positive response to the request of the Holy Spirit. To be sent out as missionaries was the culmination of a process God had begun in their lives.

Barnabas, as a Hellenistic Jew, was both multilingual and bicultural. He had grown up on the island of Cyprus where he was schooled in the ways of the Romans. He was also a Levite and would have been taught the Scriptures in the synagogue. Barnabas no doubt spoke Aramaic, Hebrew, Greek, and perhaps one of the local dialects. God would use the elements of his background to prepare him for a great missionary adventure.

Barnabas was sent out as an envoy from the church in Jerusalem to check into the happenings in the city of Antioch. His ministry resulted in the edification and establishment of a strong church, as well as the mentoring several key leaders, including Saul. His ministry in Antioch was his first missionary assignment. The events of Acts 13 which led to him being sent out with Saul were, in reality, his second missionary journey. Barnabas was a living example of someone with a missionary's passion for lost souls.

Much like Barnabas, Saul did not suddenly wake up to a missionary calling. God worked in his heart and mind to prepare him for his destiny as an apostle and spokesman for Christ. His upbringing, raised in the Roman city of Tarsus, gave him insights God would use in his evangelistic, apologetic, and preaching ministries. Ananias, the first believer to contact Saul after his conversion, told him of the prophecy God had given him about Saul. He informed Saul that he was a "chosen instrument to proclaim my name to the Gentiles and their kings" (Acts 9:15). Barnabas observed Saul's commitment to spread the Gospel in a foreign land, as seen in his willingness to leave Tarsus and go to Antioch. In Saul's life there was a growing awareness of the purposes of God—seeds that were planted long before the events of the Acts 13 prayer meeting.

God used a number of factors and people to initiate a process that prepared the soil for what I came to recognize as my own missionary calling. He used the prayers of my parents and grandmother. He taught me through many Sunday School lessons, sermons, and Bible studies. Circumstances formulated a sense of destiny that developed the sense of God's calling upon my life.

Tim Tjosvold was one of the people God used to plant the seeds of His calling upon my life.[3] Tim's exuberant and energetic love for missions was contagious. When he worked in our church, he and his wife, Brenda, were preparing to leave and serve as missionaries with our denomination to the country of Ivory Coast, West Africa. Tim's excitement and example produced fruit in the lives of many teens who ultimately found themselves also called by God to missionary service.

Tim's influence upon the youth group resulted in lives that reflected his dreams and passions. Like others in the group, I ended up like the one who was my discipler. Although he was in a different stage of realizing God's calling upon his life, Tim was one of the human vessels God used to direct my life. At the time Tim didn't imagine the changed lives that would come out of our youth group, but today there are many men and women from that group who serve God in the four corners of this world.

Ravi Zacharias, author and apologist, is another man God used in my life to plant a seed that would eventually germinate in the form of my personal calling to missions.[4] God has brought this servant into my life on a number of occasions and has used his ministry, both through the spoken and written word, in a significant way to draw me closer to Himself.

As a young boy I went to a large inter-church rally at Edmonton's Jubilee Auditorium. The sheer numbers of the 2000 people in attendance impressed me, as my family attended a small congregation. However, what stands foremost in my memory was the young, slender preacher who relayed God's message to us with passion and power. That evening, together with a myriad of others, I made a commitment to live a life that would make an impact for Christ.

Ten years later I attended a large youth event, *Life '80*, in Estes Park, Colorado. One of the keynote speakers was Ravi Zacharias, and once again God used him in my life.

On the second-to-last evening of that conference Ravi gave a challenge for the youth in attendance to present their lives as living sacrifices, to make an impact for God through their careers, ministries at the local church level, and through their families. This appealed to me as I had made my plans to go into university and study civil engineering. But God had other plans and a quiet, reassuring voice spoke to my spirit. "Not tonight. Tomorrow's your night."

With great anticipation, and perhaps a bit of fear and trembling, I entered the auditorium on the final evening of the conference. I knew God had planted the seeds of His calling and will for my life through others but this was a night of confirmation. A drama troupe presented two or three moving skits, including the one at the beginning of this chapter, *The Call*. Ravi Zacharias spoke of the need for youth to commit themselves to the task of world evangelization and missions. It was as if a shovel full of dirt came tumbling down to cover the seed that was now planted deep in my heart and soul.

Phase II: God's Call is Nurtured through Significant People and Experiences

Barnabas and Saul passed through a phase of preparation that nurtured and watered the soil of their lives. This enhanced their ability to respond to God when He finally indicated the time had come to leave Antioch. Both men sharpened and served others during this process, developing godly character and a sense of partnership. They were given the opportunity to hone their gifts and abilities in the school of practical experience. This led them to a place and time where they were willing to leave the safe and friendly confines of Antioch to go and preach the Gospel in new territory.[5]

Saul's nurturing process did not occur over a short period. There is a tendency to assume that the time between Saul's conversion and his missionary activities was a period of one or two years. But by his own testimony, he indicated he waited three years before going to Jerusalem to first meet the apostles (Galatians 1:18). At that time most were still fearful of him. He did not return to Jerusalem until fourteen years later (Galatians 2:1), which most commentators identify as the voyage mentioned in Acts 11:29-30. There would have been a minimum of two or three years that followed this trip, as both men ministered in Antioch and left on their historic missionary journey.

I may not be very good at math, but by my calculations, the time between Saul's conversion and his taking on the leadership of the ministry team in Acts 16 would be nearly twenty years. That's a far cry from the fast-track approach often equated to his ministry formation.

The preparation or nurturing phase in my life took place over a period of more than ten years, and included the influence of many different individuals. There was an educational aspect to this phase, lasting a number of years. During this time many fine professors poured their lives into me through their teaching. This phase included an aspect of practical ministry, when colleagues and mentors shared from their experience. God used a number of men and women to spur me on to healthy growth and maturity in my relationship with Him. God used these people to cast their shadow of influence upon me, teaching me to recognize His plan for my life.

Arnold Cook, missionary and former President of the Christian and Missionary Alliance in Canada, was one of many significant people God used in my life during this phase. He had a way of being bluntly honest. He got straight to the real issues in a person's life. His coy smile and approving wink became his trademark as he encouraged those under his ministry to make their "MIFG –Maximum Impact For God."[6] He left the imprint of his love for God and passion for missions upon my life.

Another person God brought into my life at this time was my wife, Rhonda. A whole book could be written about the lessons I have learned from her. She has been willing to follow her adventurous husband to different continents and nations. We have been a part of each other's growth process as we seek God's will for our lives.

One final aspect in my growth process has been the authors God used to prepare me for life and ministry. Unknown to them, authors like Josh McDowell and Ravi Zacharias have fueled my interest in apologetics. Men like James Dobson and Gary Smalley have been mentors for my marriage and family. Other men and women have inspired me with their stories of missions and world evangelism. God used all of them to enrich and enhance my life.

A person who is growing in his awareness of God's calling upon his or her life is not sitting by the wayside waiting for something to happen. As they grow in their sense of calling and direction, God uses them in the lives of others. They may not have an official title, nor be people who are in ministry on a fulltime basis, but their sensitivity to God's purposes and their desire to be used by Him do not go unnoticed.

It was during the nurture-and-growth stage of my sense of calling that I met Brad and Mark. They showed great potential in leadership and a desire to know and follow God. The initial foundation of our friendship was a love for hiking and mountaineering, but it would go to much deeper levels. As time passed, we developed a relationship that was not overtly formal, but that led to times of mentorship. We not only climbed dozens of mountains, but also spurred one another on to new spiritual heights.

Phase III: God's Call is Harvested through Obedience

The final phase of God's calling is a positive response in obedience to His direction. For Barnabas and Saul, as well in the lives of many others, this took the form of an affirmative decision to the events recorded in Acts 13. It is almost as if God gives one final opportunity to test our willingness to obediently follow Him.

Barnabas and Saul must have felt excited when the leaders of the Antioch church turned to them and said, "Well, are you willing to go?" The two men looked at each other and gave a resounding, "*Yes!*"

Barnabas and Saul seem to have anticipated such an assignment. They left Antioch with clear direction and purpose. This was a result of their times of prayer and sensitivity to the leading of the Holy Spirit.

The willingness of the Antioch church leaders to release the two men for this ministry not only served to confirm this decision, but it also released them to pursue new horizons. This was a commendable action on their part. Most leaders would probably look for someone who wasn't quite as involved or quite so important to the ministry of their local church. Unafraid to send out their best, the Antioch leaders affirmed Barnabas and Saul in this decision.

Barnabas, who responded positively when requested to go to Antioch as Jerusalem's envoy, was selected to be the leader. The first stop in their itinerary took the two men to Cyprus, Barnabas' homeland. He had gone through a process in which God had prepared him for this ministry, and now he was ready to respond.

Saul's positive response to the leading of the Spirit is best understood when we consider his clear and specific calling from the first moments of his conversion. Ananias related to him the Lord's instruction, telling Saul of God's plans for his life. He was a chosen instrument to carry the Gospel to the Gentiles and their kings (Acts 9:15). The events of Saul's life, combined with his calling, prepared him and led to this moment.

Barnabas and Saul's decision was emphatic. Their bags were packed and they were on their way to Cyprus in a short time. This was a natural step of obedience for them, affirming God's call and work in their lives.

Rhonda and I experienced a similar situation as we came to a point of decision and obedience in our lives. We were invited by a church to come on staff as the assistant pastor for youth. It was an opportunity that included the chance to work with a respected young pastor and his wife. We were finishing our studies at seminary and were tempted by the generous salary offered. We knew the church, loved the people, and would have been happy to accept their proposal.

We asked for a week to pray and think things over because there was only one possible situation that held us back from giving an immediate "yes" to their request: we both sensed we were called to prepare for missions and needed to consider whether this would impede our future departure once we finally did receive "the call." The church leadership graciously accepted our request to pray and think through the implications of their offer. They applauded our desire to be 100% sure of God's direction for our lives.

We didn't need a week to discover God's will. The next morning the phone rang. The Assistant to the Director of Missions Personnel was on the other end of the line. "We've been looking over your file and see you want to go to Brazil. Is that still the case?" she asked. It had been years since we had applied and in that time we had not heard a word from the missions office. In a few short moments we were setting up an appointment with the director. This was the first step in the final process that took us to

Brazil. God's *kairos* timing was evident to us—the culmination of years of preparation and sensing His calling upon our lives.

Just why God places a final step of obedience in response to His call upon our lives, I do not know. Perhaps it's like the icing on the cake or the cherry on the ice cream float. The final step of obedience is something that concretizes the preparation and process leading to the final moment of accepting God's direction. Perhaps the final step of obedience seals a covenant in our souls to commit ourselves to hear His voice and follow His leading.

———

When I reflect upon the lives of Barnabas and Saul, comparing them to my personal journey, I see there is a process common to people who are seeking to do God's will. There is a phase of conception, or planting, where the person has a sense of "perhaps this is the direction I should take." This is followed by a period of growth and preparation God uses to nurture His calling upon their lives. There is a final step of obedience, leaving all other options behind and going ahead with confidence that this is indeed the direction of God. This begins a lifelong journey of following and obeying God. It can take years to see its fulfillment, but once started, this is the process God uses to direct His followers.

A disciple becomes like his mentor. Barnabas and Saul were not the exception. Saul took Barnabas' example to heart and followed in his footsteps, becoming a man who was marked by his sensitivity to the leading of the Holy Spirit.

Those under the care of a mentor are on a journey of discovery. Wise mentors are able to help their disciples learn God's general will as revealed in the Scriptures. They model a constant seeking of God for His direction in their own lives. They are growing in their sense of destiny and calling, preparing themselves as they seek God. They model the steps of obedience which lead to a confirmation and acknowledgment of God's will in their lives. They don't only teach principles; they live them. This is God's way of changing the world.

Study Guide

ACTIVE LEARNING ...

In groups of two or three, complete the following activity and then present your work to the larger group.

1. Make a timeline of Paul's life, listing the events of the book of Acts in chronological order. Mark the two most significant experiences in his life with a lightning bolt.

Macedonian Call	Jerusalem Council
Ministry in Antioch	Road to Damascus
Stoning of Stephen	Rejected in Jerusalem
Trial before Festus	Stoning in Lystra
Jailed in Philippi	Prayer of Ananias
Invited by Barnabas	Voyage to Rome

2. Why did you or your group chose the two events as the most significant events in Paul's life? What changed in his life as a result of each experience? What principles of seeking and knowing God's will are exemplified by Paul?

CONSIDER ...

Read Exodus 2:1-10; 3:1-22, and 4:1-17. The three phases of knowing and affirming God's direction in a leader's life can be observed in the life of Moses. Answer the following questions, taking into account other information you know of the life of Moses.

1. In what way was the call of God planted, nurtured, and harvested in Moses?

2. Who were the significant people God used to affirm Moses' sense of destiny?

3. What are the similarities between the calling of Moses and Paul?

RESPOND ...

Principle: Knowing and affirming God's will is a lifelong process.

1. What are the seeds of God's calling upon your life? At what point in your spiritual journey did you begin to sense God's divine guidance?

2. How have you been nurtured during your maturing process? Who are the people or what are the circumstances which have resulted in the greatest growth in your life?

3. What is one step of obedience you took to seal an affirmation of God's calling upon your life? How can you use this experience to help other people better understand God's will and direction in their lives?

CHAPTER 7
HOME IS WHERE THE SUITCASE IS

There's never a dull moment at our home, wherever it may be. My wife and I have lived in three countries, ten cities, and fifteen different houses. At the moment we're not anticipating a move to a new city, or a new home, but you never know when that might happen. With all of our moving and travel commitments there's rarely a moment when a suitcase isn't being either packed or unpacked. This has been a fact of life for my wife and I ever since we were married.

With all the changes we've faced we are often asked, "Where do you call home?" The long answer we give is that we're committed to God's guidance and need to make our home wherever He leads us. The short answer we often offer is, "Home is where the suitcase is."

In the midst of a mobile life it has been important to establish a sense of belonging for our family. There is a need to have a place where we can rest, be ourselves, and just crash. This is a place where we are comfortable, not facing the challenges and pressures of daily life. Our home becomes a personal retreat center where we can recharge our physical and spiritual batteries, receiving clear direction from God.

Any time I move into a new setting, it is important for me to determine two places of refuge, which in most cases are in different parts of the house. I need a special spot in a comfortable chair where I can sit each day to read and pray. This place is generally located away from the hustle and bustle of the kitchen, but close enough so coffee refills don't distract from what I'm reading. I also need a desk or office space where I can write, plan, and work. I am never really at home until those two places have been established.

There's a wonderful feeling, especially after traveling or being away for some days, when I come back to those two places. The sigh of relief I breathe is an expression of contentment and comfort: "This is where I belong."

The same sense of belonging can be felt in my personal ministry. There are times when I am comfortable with what I am doing and receive a true sense of fulfillment. I may even find myself telling others, "This is what God made me to be," or "This is God's calling upon my life." The journey I took to arrive at this conclusion is what I would like to share in this chapter.

The process of spiritual gift discovery and development Barnabas and Saul followed is remembered by Church history as the first missionary voyage. Both men grew in their knowledge and employment of their gifts during their travels. In two short chapters their roles and responsibilities are defined. This is highlighted by Saul's name change, as he is referred to as Paul from this point forward in the Scriptures.[1] At the end of their journey, the two men are truly at home with who they are and with what God called them to do. It's almost as if they returned from their long trip, sat down in a familiar chair, and breathed a deep sigh of relief.

Spiritual Gift Discovery and Development

The first missionary journey, recorded Acts 13 and 14, was marked by the presence and ministry of the Holy Spirit in and through the lives of Barnabas and Paul. They were set apart and sent out by the Holy Spirit, accomplishing God's purposes and spreading the good news of Jesus Christ (Acts 13:2-4). They followed God's leading as they visited Jews and Greeks in the cities of Cyprus and Asia Minor.

In some places the two were welcomed, the crowds listening with interest to their message and desiring to learn more of Christ. Barnabas and Paul were also persecuted and encountered strong opposition, something they would face with joy and a renewed sense of the filling of the Holy Spirit (Acts 13:52). Their boldness in preaching, confirmed by miraculous signs and wonders, established numerous churches (Acts 13:6-12, 14:3 and 14:8-10). Many people were won over to the faith (Acts 14:21).

Then Barnabas and Paul then retraced their steps through Asia Minor to encourage the newly formed groups of believers, appointing elders and leaders (Acts 14:21-23). All of this was the result of the leading and working of the Holy Spirit in and through their lives.

At the onset of their journey, Barnabas was the clear leader. His name is mentioned first as the Holy Spirit requested the Church leaders to "set apart for me Barnabas and Saul for the work to which I have called them"

(Acts 13:2). The initial stop in their travels took them to Cyprus, the birthplace of Barnabas. Their ministry was to preach as they went throughout the island (Acts 13:4-12). Barnabas followed the principle that Jesus mapped out for His disciples in Acts 1:8, as he took the Gospel first to his personal Jerusalem. His knowledge of the island and its inhabitants made him the primary candidate to head up this missionary venture.

The event leading to Saul's promotion as chief spokesperson, as well as to the broad acceptance of his name change, reveals a recognition of spiritual giftedness on the part of both men. There was a fresh filling of the Holy Spirit when Saul fixed his eyes upon the sorcerer, Bar-Jesus, and denounced him for what he was; "a child of the devil and an enemy of everything that is right...full of all kinds of deceit and trickery" (Acts 13:10). Now called Paul, the disciple formerly known as Paul experienced his prophetic gifting coming to the forefront. He saw things as either black or white and boldly declared his message. These are the first recorded words of Paul. Two previous passages talk of his preaching in the synagogues of Damascus (Acts 9:20) and his open proclamation in Jerusalem (Acts 9:28), but do not record the actual discourse.

Barnabas took a step back as Paul addressed the evil spirit. From this point forward there is a name change and a shift of focus in Paul's ministry.

Paul's ministry as an apologist and public speaker began to flourish. His first recorded sermon, delivered in the synagogue in Antioch Pisidian, is a defense of the person and work of Jesus Christ (Acts 13:16-41). He spoke to the Jews about their rejection of Christ as the Promised One and declared Jesus as the Savior of all people. This discourse challenged his hearers to consider the evidence of Christ's fulfillment of prophecy, His life and acts while on earth, and the need for each person to respond to His claims. It led to active discussion among Jewish and Gentile leaders, and eventually to the expulsion of Barnabas and Paul from the city. The Jewish leadership clearly did not want to deal with the popularity the two missionaries were generating.

The pattern Paul and Barnabas developed in Acts 13 and 14 became the trademark of their future ministries. They began by visiting the Jewish synagogue of the city, speaking of Jesus as the Messiah. They went on to speak to the Gentile population, proclaiming Christ as the chosen sacrifice for all people and all nations. This generally sparked envy in the hearts of the Jewish leaders and led to persecution. Such was the case in Iconium and Lystra, two of the stopovers on the itinerary of the first missionary journey.

Barnabas did not relinquish his role as team strategist and leader throughout their travels. This was a ministry in which he flourished. This can be seen in how the two men were perceived by their hearers. Acts 14:12 records the events in Lystra, where Barnabas was identified as Zeus, the primary Greek god and hearer of the people's prayers.[2] Paul was the preacher of the team and was thought to be Hermes, the spokesman of Zeus.[3] Inhabitants of the city wanted to offer sacrifices to the men whom they believed were Greek gods come down from the heavens. The ensuing confusion led to a riot and the expulsion of Barnabas and Paul from the city. This event, which occurred in the second-to-last city Barnabas and Paul visited, highlighted each man's principal role and function in their partnership.

Barnabas continued to encourage others; Acts 14:22 is a description of his ministry. This had not changed over the years, as Acts 11:23 speaks of his goal to strengthen the faith of people, preparing them for the problems and persecution he knew they would face. Under Barnabas' leadership the two men retraced their steps and visited the new believers in the cities of Asia Minor. The caring and nurturing nature of Barnabas once again stood out as the outstanding aspect of his personal ministry.

There are three great lessons to glean from Barnabas and Paul's journey of discovery and development of their spiritual gifts. The implications of what they learned apply to the Church to this day.

First, spiritual gifts are given to individuals for specific purposes, roles, and ministries. They often match the calling and personality of their receiver, enabling a person to be the person God wants them to be. They come to the forefront as a person is active in ministry situations, though they can be latent for a period of time. Gifts are given to serve God's purposes and designs, not those of the individual.

Second, spiritual gifts are confirmed and observed by the Church and others, including non-believers. The church in Antioch recognized apostolic gifting in the lives of Barnabas and Saul, and thus sent them out (Acts 13:1-3). The Cyprian governor Sergio Paulus was astonished by Paul's miraculous powers and prophetic message, and received the Gospel (Acts 13:6-12). The people of Lystra recognized Barnabas' leadership and Paul's speaking abilities, although wrongly identifying them as Greek gods (Acts 14:8-13). The spiritual gifts of Paul and Barnabas were confirmed by others, giving them a green light to further develop and employ these gifts in their ministries.

Finally, confirmation of spiritual giftedness comes through fruitfulness and a sense of satisfaction in ministry. The process of Acts 13 and 14 left Paul and Barnabas comfortable with their roles in ministry. Paul stepped forward with a renewed calling and boldness to proclaim the Gospel to the Gentiles. Barnabas went on to disciple and restore Mark, a task that would result in the first written account of the life of Christ. There was an acceptance of their destinies after the events of the inaugural missionary journey. Both men could affirm: "This is where I belong!"

Acts 14 ends with a missionary conference where Paul and Barnabas reported what God had done in them and through them. They rejoiced in the spreading of the Gospel to new cities and nations. As instruments in His hands, they spoke of the work God had accomplished. Their vivid declaration confirmed God's role in the work, equipping them and filling them with the Holy Spirit.

Benefits of Gift-Based Ministry

God's design for believers as they make an impact upon the world is to work out of His equipping and filling. He gives the Holy Spirit to each follower, and imparts spiritual gifts and ministries which are to be used for the glory of God. When God works through chosen human vessels, there are great spiritual blessings and lasting transformations in the lives of people.

One of the immediate benefits from ministry that flows out of the proper use of the spiritual gifts is the effective edification of the Church. The lives of people, who are the "living stones" (1 Peter 2:5) and the primary material of the Church's make-up, are transformed when ministries depend upon the power of the Holy Spirit.[4] Too often the debate about the use of certain gifts totally sidesteps this revealed purpose of the gifts, which are given to either bring people into a new relationship with God or to deepen a person's walk with Him. Teaching about the spiritual gifts should result in a stronger, Christ-centered Church. Spiritual gifts are given to help the Church fulfill its role as a life-giving organism used by God to transform the world.

A second important aspect of gift-based ministry is God's reconfirmation of His calling in the lives of individuals. There is great joy when one can see God's stamp of approval upon a ministry. This affirmation underlines God's purposes as He uses individuals to fill specific roles within the work of building up the Church. This often leads to a recognition and deeper dependence upon the Holy Spirit to empower and work through individuals.

The focal point of gift-based ministry is not the receiver of the spiritual gift, but rather the Giver. The attitude of Paul and Barnabas in Acts 14:22-27 reflected this viewpoint, as they did not say, "Look what we did." Instead their emphasis was on what God had done in them and through them. Individuals who have the correct focus and use their gifts for God's glory echo this affirmation.

Gift-based ministry eliminates an unhealthy comparison between individuals. Each person's spiritual gifts are to be used in conjunction with the gifts of others. This complements and multiplies effectiveness in ministry, and should not lead to competition with fellow workers. No single person can experience the fullness and effectiveness which working with others can accomplish.

Avoiding The Comparison Game

One of the obstacles I had to overcome in my own ministry is what I call the "comparison game." Others aptly call this the "performance treadmill." The idea is the same, as the focus on what I did for God overshadowed what He called me to be. As a result, I began to measure myself against the abilities or successes of others.

As a young missionary I compared myself to Sanford Hashimoto, a Japanese-American colleague in Brazil. He is perhaps the most gifted personal evangelist I know. His ability to explain the Gospel and lead people to Christ made him a role model worth emulating. Those who know Sanford say that, given enough time, he could convert a telephone pole.

A problem began to surface as I compared Sanford's strengths in the area of evangelism with my weaknesses. It didn't help when he would pray that I would become a soul-winner. His weekly reports of those who had accepted Christ as Savior began to grate on me. I longed to be like him, but all my efforts in the area of personal evangelism fell short of my expectations.

If only I could be like Sanford, I thought as I began to make comparisons. *Sanford has slain his thousands, but I've . . . well, that's a different story! Shouldn't I have more than the small handful of souls won for Christ? What kind of a Christian am I anyway? If I were a real missionary, wouldn't I be more like him?*

The mind-game I played led to a destructive, downward spiral. I wasn't only jealous of my colleague, but I found myself making unhealthy comparisons that resulted in a critical spirit. This caused me to focus on all of my shortcomings, instead of accepting who God had gifted me to be. I tried to be like Sanford Hashimoto, but found I was having enough problems just being me.

One of the people who helped me get out of this comparison trap was Wendie, Sanford's wife. She is not an evangelist by nature, but rather is another who comes alongside and disciples new converts. I saw how this couple worked in unison to achieve the same goal: to present every person as a mature believer and follower of Christ (Colossians 1:28). I learned a great lesson from Sanford and Wendie Hashimoto, as together they made a great missionary team, winning people to Christ and building them up in their faith.

I am not an evangelist by my spiritual gifting, but my skills are needed by those who reach out to others. This does not absolve me of the responsibility of personal evangelism, but it does free me from comparisons that can bind and hinder me from carrying out the tasks for which I know God has gifted me. If I am content to be the person God has called me to be, and indeed gifted me to be, I don't have to compare myself to others. Rather, I can seek to complement that person's areas of weakness.

Most evangelists are not natural disciple-makers. Those who win people to Christ often struggle with the tasks of teaching basic truths and helping new converts to apply them to their lives. They need someone to help complete the task of building the new person up in the faith, forming mature believers. God's intention is not for the two types of people to compete with each other. They are to work to complement the other's ministry and area of giftedness.

I learned two important truths as I stopped focusing on the differences of gifting and began to work to complement my team member. Evangelism without discipleship is irresponsible. Discipleship which does not lead to evangelism lacks vision and understanding of what it means to be a true follower of Christ. These two areas of ministry do not compete against each other, but are complementary. Individuals gifted in these areas need to work together, allowing God to use their gifts to accomplish the tasks of evangelism and discipleship in the lives of new believers.

Paul reaffirms this truth in his first letter to the Corinthian church when he states,

> I planted the seed, Apollos watered it, but God has been making it grow. So neither the one who plants nor the one who waters is anything, but only God, who makes things grow. (1 Corinthians 3:6-7)

God will use different people during different phases of a person's spiritual growth. Paul concluded that both of those involved in this process are equally important and dependent upon God. Paul considered Apollos as one who complemented his ministry. He also acknowledged God's role and design in all of this, resulting in a transformation of the lives of those whom he had reached.

Paul's practical lesson showed him that interdependence with others who have different spiritual gifts is a key to healthy churches and mature disciples. It is also a key to avoiding the comparison game.

When I finally realized that it was okay for me to be me and that I didn't have to strive to be someone else, I discovered a new freedom in ministry. I began to celebrate my differences from others as something God used to add effectiveness in our efforts to win people to Christ and plant new churches. I could rejoice with them in their victories, and lend a hand when my gifts warranted.

God will use a number of different individuals to win, build, and equip the person who follows Him. Nobody is gifted in every area of ministry or able to complete each task in the life of a new believer. Each one needs the other to complement their areas of weakness. As a team we become stronger and more effective as we allow others to take on responsibilities that require their spiritual gifts. The two go hand in hand, and don't compete with each other. Each individual's responsibility is to find out where they fit into this task and to work together with those around them.

Your ministry and role in the Church is not only important, but it is a vital part of what God is doing to build his Kingdom in your town or city. Every part of the body, however insignificant it may appear, has a vital role to play. This is true in the physical and spiritual realms. Just ask the Spanish soccer star, Santiago Cañizares.

In the build-up to the 2002 World Cup, it was announced that Santiago Cañizares would be the starting goalkeeper for the aspiring Spanish national team. But then, his hopes to play on Spain's national team were dashed one fateful evening, two weeks before the start of the tournament. In a quick mishap, a cologne bottle fell from a bathroom sink, shattered, and severed the tendon of his big toe. Although this was not a life-threatening injury, it was reason enough for Santiago Cañizares to be scratched from the line-up of his country's squad. Instead of going to Korea and Japan as a star goalkeeper he would have to watch the World Cup from the sidelines.[5]

Scriptures teach us that every part of the body is important—even the big toe. Similarly, in the Church, each person has a significant role in what God is doing to build His Kingdom. As Paul states in Romans 12:3, "Do not think of yourself more highly than you ought." Nor should anyone think less of themselves, as all members of the Body of Christ have a vital and important role to play.

Disciples who recognize their individual giftedness and role within the Church can begin to minister with great freedom. They can accept and invite those with different spiritual gifts to come alongside them and touch others. This freedom gives a sense of being at home in their lives and personal ministries, acknowledging this as part of God's design and purpose for their lives.

Study Guide

ACTIVE LEARNING ...

1. Read 1 Corinthians 3:5-9. Use the words of Paul as an example (verse 6) to fill in the blanks with three people who have influenced your spiritual life.

    _____ planted the seed, _____ watered it, and _____ helped it to grow.

2. Form groups of two or three. In your group, share the phrase you wrote. What spiritual gift(s) did each of these people employ as they made an impact for God upon your life?

CONSIDER ...

1. Carefully read Acts Chapters 13 and 14, noting references to the ministry of Barnabas and Paul. Use the example below to make a list of references of spiritual gifts, the people involved, and the resulting ministry.

    Reference: Acts 13:1-3
    Gift Used: Discernment
    Person(s):   Barnabas, Paul and Antioch leaders
    Result: The two men were set apart and sent on their way to preach the Gospel.

2. Compare the list you developed in question 1 with the spiritual gifts listed in Romans 12:6-8 and Ephesians 4:11. Which gift(s) did Barnabas display? In what areas does Paul stand out? How did the two men complement each other?

3. Why did the roles of Barnabas and Paul change during their journey? What were the results when each man worked in areas of his spiritual gifting?

RESPOND ...

Principle: There is a sense of freedom with no need to compare oneself to others when a person is ministering within the areas of their spiritual gifts.

1. Identify one spiritual gift God has given you. How has God used this gift in the past? What areas of ministry are best suited for this gift? How are you able to minister in ways that others cannot minister?

2. What are you doing to discover and develop your spiritual gifts? Write a prayer which thanks God for your spiritual gift(s), dedicating them for His use and purposes.

CHAPTER 8
THEY SPELLED MY NAME WRONG!

I couldn't believe my eyes. *Not again*, I thought as I folded the paper, my misspelled name jumping from the rest of the text. *How could a people who worked closely with me make a mistake like this? This really bugs me!*

The program in my hands listed the participants and organizers for the *JESUS* film project in our city. It thanked each person for their contribution to the inter-church event. I didn't know who *Duen Bueller* was, but I did recognize a sense of resentment beginning to swell up within me. The least they could have done was to check with me before taking the program to the printers.

I should have been used to it. I've lived in countries where I constantly deal with the misspelling of my name, as it does not exist in Portuguese or Spanish. The two words with a pronunciation closest to my name in Portuguese are *duende*, which means dwarf, and *doente*, the word used for "sick to the point of throwing up." What kind of parent would give their child such a name? There were times of frustration when I would say my name was *José da Silva*. Not a soul who stared back at me ever believed it.

The choice before me was to let this unintentional misspelling bother me, or to take it in stride. The situation could have been worse, for at least I knew in this case they were referring to me. There was a lesson to be learned so I swallowed hard and smiled.

There are many people who make a lasting and powerful impact for God who never see their name up in lights. Few recall the name of Mordecai Fowler Ham, the traveling preacher God used to lead a young man named Billy Graham to the Lord.[1] Does anyone remember Edward D.

Kimball, the Sunday School teacher who placed his hand upon the shoulder of a young shoe salesman, Dwight L. Moody, and prayed for his salvation?[2] Would Fanny J. Crosby have written her hymns if it had not been for her grandmother, Eunice Crosby, who read the Scriptures and encouraged her to attend the New York School for the Blind?[3] Each of these unsung heroes played an important role in the life of a person who rose to fame within the Christian community.

Barnabas, like the people mentioned above, learned to be content with second billing. Although he was the unquestionable leader of the first missionary journey, his role as the main public speaker ended at a point described in the early verses of Acts 13.

There are a number of observations to make as Barnabas and Saul made this transition in their ministry focus. Barnabas understood that a person called to be a servant-leader learns to place others first. He knew the importance of being the person God gifted him to be and learned not to compare himself to or compete with Paul. He also allowed the final evaluation of his ministry to rest with God who judges a person's service by their motivation, not necessarily by their visible results (2 Corinthians 10:12).

Changing Roles for Paul and Barnabas

Under the direction of the Holy Spirit, church leaders in Antioch set apart Barnabas and Saul for the work to which they had been called (Acts 13:2). Barnabas and Saul set sail for Cyprus, traveling and preaching the Word of God as they crossed the island. Upon arrival in Paphos, the two men were summoned by the Roman ruler, the Proconsul Sergius Paulus (Acts 13:7). The order of their names refers to Barnabas as the leader of the ministry team at the beginning of their journey.

Three significant changes take place in the narrative recorded in Acts 13:9. These changes led to a dramatic reversal of roles between the two men, when the duo known as Barnabas and Saul became known as Paul and Barnabas.

First, the defense of the Gospel to the Roman Proconsul is the background by which we are informed of Saul's other name (Acts 13:9-12). From this point forward he is referred to as Paul. It was no coincidence that Paul would address Sergius Paulus, as their common name gave the two men a basis from which to proceed. Paul, whose name means "small," would stand in opposition before the Proconsul's personal spiritual guide, Bar-Jesus, whose name means "the one who opposes." The smallness of Paul only served to underline the power of God when the sorcerer was struck blind for his belligerent behavior. From this point on we know nothing of Saul (which means the "called one") but rather Paul, the "small one," who relied on the greatness of his God.[4]

Second, Paul's address to Sergius Paulus is his first recorded discourse. Earlier passages do not record the words of either Barnabas or Saul in Antioch. Paul now stepped onto the platform as a confident and powerful preacher and became the chief spokesman of the missionary team from this point forward. He may not have necessarily have taken on the role of leader in the sense of planning and making decisions, but he was "promoted" to the position of keynote speaker. Paul's ministry to kings and rulers, speaking the message of God, had begun.

Finally, a third important factor recorded in Acts 13:9 is Paul's renewed experience of the filling of the Holy Spirit. This was the not his first encounter with the things of the Spirit, as his conversion (Acts 9:3-18) and his missionary calling (13:1-3) both indicate the Spirit's work in his life. However, something happened to Paul here, and he was changed forever. His boldness and courage as he spoke to rulers and leaders became the defining characteristic of his ministry.

As Paul stepped forward, Barnabas took a step backward and accepted a behind-the-scenes role. He did not disappear, but later he would quietly support another person's ministry; that of John-Mark. His importance as a leader was not diminished, as on two future occasions he took on a key public role. It was Barnabas who spoke up when he and Paul refused to accept worship from the crowds in Lystra (Acts 14:14). Barnabas was the first person to be heard in Jerusalem when he and Paul defended their ministry to the Gentiles (Acts 15:12). However, after Acts 13:7, the mention of Barnabas decreases while mentions of Paul increase.

There is no indication of Barnabas' feelings or reactions to this shift in roles. He seemed to take everything in stride. He not only facilitated this change, but made a personal shift of priorities that indicated his willingness to promote Paul's preaching and teaching ministries.

I can't help but wonder what went through Barnabas' mind as Paul took the floor and began to speak, fearlessly addressing the Proconsul. Perhaps his mind flashed back fifteen or sixteen years earlier when they had stood in front of the frightened Jerusalem church leaders. He may have thought of the trip to Tarsus when he searched for Saul. He might have remembered the first sermon or Scripture reading Saul undertook as he began to help in the Antioch church, stumbling over words as he took on new responsibilities. He probably sat speechless, quietly observing all that was now taking place.

This was no surprise to Barnabas. He knew of the prophecies concerning Paul. Barnabas was a tool in the hands of God, the master craftsman who had used his life to mold another man who was now promoted to new ministries and responsibilities. He wasn't bothered by this shift of priorities, nor did he allow it to become a source of envy. Barnabas would soon move on to influencing the life of another person.

Mark, one of the young men I discipled, serves as an example of this principle. Mark followed in my footsteps and studied at the same Bible college. When he came to the college, I introduced him to my friends. His outgoing personality helped him make many friends and he was a popular student. He was elected president of the student council in his senior year. He was active in many up-front activities and was well known and liked. After graduation he accepted a position as a youth pastor, and his ministries thrived. He and his wife served many years in a country closed to conventional missionary activity. All the while I've proudly watched him develop from the sidelines.

I hope you don't mind my "holy bragging" about Mark. I'm not jealous of him. I'm thankful I was allowed to play an important role in his spiritual development. He's had an effective ministry. He's gone places and done things I couldn't have imagined doing. However, in a way I'm there with him every step of the journey. This gives me a sense of pride and accomplishment, knowing my impact on the life of one person has multiplied itself to others.

Barnabas was not reluctant to promote his disciple. It is the same paradox in Jesus' teaching about a student not being greater than his master. But Barnabas did not struggle with Paul's growth as a competent leader. Rather, Barnabas seemed to thrive and rejoice in the success of his disciple. He would soon move on to another disciple, parting ways with Paul and doing what he did best: having an impact upon the life of John-Mark and changing the world a life at a time.[6]

Spiritual Greatness: What did Jesus teach?

Greatness in God's Kingdom, according to Jesus, is associated with servanthood and not self-promotion. He said:

Whoever wants to become great among you must be your servant, and whoever wants to be first must be your slave—just as the Son of Man did not come to be served, but to serve, and to give his life as a ransom for many. (Matthew 20:26-28)

Jesus not only taught servanthood as a sign of spiritual greatness, but He displayed it through His example. John's description of Jesus washing the feet of His disciples is perhaps the most explicit and moving record of Jesus' servant heart. Jesus, "taking the very nature of a servant" (Philippians 2:7), literally lowered Himself to do tasks that would not be expected from a teacher or master. There was no difference between what He said and what He did.

"You call me 'Teacher' and 'Lord,' and rightly so, for that is what
I am. Now that I, your Lord and Teacher, have washed your feet,
you also should wash one another's feet. I have set you an
example that you should do as I have done for you."

(John 13:13-15)

The disciples, who often jostled for positions and privileges, had not learned this lesson. It went against their nature. They were jealous of each other. Their relatives even got involved, approaching Jesus and asking Him for favors He could not grant. Their story reads like a corporate struggle for power, not like that of a group of people who wanted to change the world through a revolution of love and service.

At times the attitude of self-promotion creeps into my life. It *does* bother me when my name is misspelled or credit is given to another. There are times when I wish that I didn't have to be the one to give up my rights. Even though I know that Jesus wants to see a servant's heart in His followers, I struggle with attitudes that well up from within me and I don't want to comply with this teaching. Like Paul in Romans 7, I know what I ought to do, but I just don't feel like doing it.

As with other aspects of the Christian life, I need to acknowledge that the attitudes and actions God desires are not natural to my human nature or character. I need to come to the end of my rope of self-effort and cry out, "I can't do this! If things are ever going to change, You'll have to live in me and through me." It is only as I seek God's transforming power that this tension can be overcome.

Barnabas, if not present at the Passover celebration with Jesus, was certainly aware of Jesus washing the disciples' feet. The traditional location of this Last Supper was the house of Mary, who was the mother of Mark and a close relative of Barnabas (Acts 12:12).[6] Even if he was not present, Barnabas lived a life that took to heart the example and command Jesus gave His followers. It was also the work of the Holy Spirit producing Christ's character in his life.

The description of Acts 11:24 reveals how Barnabas was able to put others first. Barnabas "was a good man, full of the Holy Spirit and faith." It was the fullness of the indwelling Holy Spirit that produced Christ-like character in Barnabas This was his secret!

I am cautious of those who claim to be followers of Christ, but who do not display evidence of a servant-like attitude or the fruit of the Holy Spirit. They do not heed the complete teaching of the filling of the Holy Spirit (Ephesians 5:18, Colossians 3:12, and Romans 8:9). These commands are followed by the description of a Spirit-controlled life (Ephesians 5:19-6:9, Colossians 3:13-4:6, and Romans 8:10-17). Those who do not give attention to Christ-likeness in the lives of His followers are like wolves in sheep's clothing. As Paul states in 2 Timothy 3:5, such people have "a form of godliness but deny its power", and concluding "Have nothing to do with such people."

This is one of the paradoxes of the Scriptures. Greatness is measured in servanthood. God's power can only truly be seen in our weakness (2 Corinthians 12:9). God's glory is transmitted in jars of clay (2 Corinthians 4:7). The world can be changed one life at a time.

Servant Leadership versus Leadership's Servant

A problem faced when teaching principles of servant leadership is the common misunderstanding of what it means to be a servant-leader. This person is not a doormat, used and abused by those with other gifts, running around and filling their orders. Their service to God and role in the lives of others represents a high calling which is a vital part of the body of Christ.

The New Testament teaches that, as we serve others, we are offering service directly to God. Jesus emphasized obedience to God, accomplishing all the Father had asked Him to do (John 14:31; 17:4). Paul's teaching on masters and servants indicated the importance of sincerity of heart and reverence for God, because we work for the Lord and not for people (Colossians 3:22-25). Acts of service, charity, and kindness unseen by people in this world do not go unnoticed by God, and will be rewarded in heaven. They culminate in the expression of the Father saying, "Whatever you did for one of the least of these brothers and sisters of mine, you did for me" (Matthew 25:40).

Three of the words Paul used to describe himself in the introductory sections of his epistles speak of servant-like attitudes. He called himself an apostle, a prisoner of the Lord, and a servant. While the office of apostle is elevated in today's thinking, its original meaning is "a sent one" or "commissary." This person does not speak for themselves, but represents another. All three terms had negative connotations to Paul's readers, representing obedience, humiliation, and submission.

This is a flip-flop from what is considered "normal" for leaders in many circles. Even the disciples who watched Jesus' example didn't understand the principle of serving others. History reveals struggles for position and power that have continued to plague the Church. Some of today's leadership gurus preach a dogma of self-exertion, success, and control. There has been a lack of biblical understanding and a rejection of Jesus' definition of a godly leader—one who welcomes using the towel and the basin, faithfully serving others.

In Spanish-speaking churches there is a saying: "*El que no sirve, no sirve!*" The verb *servir* has two meanings: "to serve" and "to be useful." The phrase literally means "The one who doesn't serve is not useful." This is especially true of leaders who forget to make the service to others their trademark.

Paul used the same wordplay in Philemon 1:10-11, when he speaks of Onesimus, the runaway slave. The name Onesimus means "useful." Paul writes, "…he was useless to you, but now he has become useful both to you and to me." Paul elevated the position of servanthood when he encouraged Philemon to receive Onesimus, no longer as a possession or slave, but as a "dear brother" (Philemon 1:16).

It is important to understand the high calling represented in service to others. Shortly after Jesus gave the wonderful example of washing the disciples feet, He said:

> "I no longer call you servants, because a servant does not know his master's business. Instead, I have called you friends, for everything that I learned from my Father I have made known to you." (John 15:15)

One who serves others is called a friend and brother of God. Such a person is a leader of impact, not just someone to be used or sought out by leadership. Although he or she may not receive immediate recognition, Jesus taught that this person will hear the words; "Well done, good and faithful servant. You have been faithful with a few things; I will put you in charge of many things. Come and share your master's happiness" (Matthew 25:23).

The Richness of a Good Name

At first glance it appears Barnabas left no legacy in the New Testament, with little or no recognition given to his mentoring ministry. However, when I read the description of Barnabas as the "son of encouragement" and "as a good man, full of the Holy Spirit and faith," I realize he left a good name which is a rich inheritance.

The Scriptures teach the great worth of a good name. "A good name is more desirable than great riches; to be esteemed is better than silver or gold" (Proverbs 22:1). "A good name is better than fine perfume," says Ecclesiastes 7:1. While this is not easily measured, it is also not bought at a bargain-basement price. A good name is something earned over time. It represents a legacy that can be made through a life given in service to God and others.

Paul does not make note of the important role of Barnabas in his life. He mentions his mentor only three times. One of these references casually states that Mark, the cousin of Barnabas, is also a prisoner with him (Colossians 4:10). The second chapter of Galatians mentions Barnabas twice. One of these references has a negative tone, portraying Barnabas as one who was nearly led astray by the hypocrisy of the legalistic Jews. There is a striking lack of any positive comment or recognition of Barnabas.

In fairness to Paul, it needs to be stated that he was not one to look for credit, nor apparently to give credit to anyone except to God. What mattered to Paul was the growth of God's Kingdom and exalting His name. Luke would be the one to paint a bright picture of the lasting legacy and good name left behind by Barnabas.

A friend who helped me understand the concept of the worth of a good name is Brian Bowen. A retired police officer, Brian and his wife Norma came to Brazil to help set up the city-wide, evangelistic event mentioned in the opening paragraphs of this chapter. They used the *JESUS* film as a rallying point that united many churches. [8]

I heard Brian say, "God delights to work when we're not worried about who gets the credit." He was not concerned about getting the glory for himself, nor for his organization. His primary purpose was to glorify God.

This attitude can be contrasted with that of a colleague who once told me on the subject of an interdenominational project, "I don't mind you working on this event, but we have to get something out of it!" He didn't realize the worth of a good name, and was worried about who got the credit.

———————

As I watched the proceedings and heard the testimonies of all God had done, I folded the program in my hands. I set aside my right to recognition and thanked God for His wonderful work in bringing together churches and leaders. I joined the choruses of *Gloria a Deus!*—Glory to God!—that filled the room. Something much more important was happening, and even if they did spell my name wrong, I didn't want to miss out on it.

Behind every hero of the faith are a myriad of men and women who were used by God to shape and form the character of their disciples. These unsung heroes make an impact upon the world that will only be fully appreciated in heaven.

Study Guide

ACTIVE LEARNING ...

The film industry reserves special recognition for actors and actresses who fill supporting roles. While these people were not considered the stars of the film, their contribution added to the overall impact of the production. Form small groups and complete the following:

1. Make a list of three actors or actresses whose supporting role contributed to the success of a film. What was the part they played and how did it enrich the final production?

2. Make a second list of three Bible personalities you would nominate for the award of "Best Supporting Character." What was their contribution to the story? How were they used by God in the life of the main character?

Share your two lists with the larger group.

CONSIDER ...

1. Compare the teaching of the Proverbs (Proverbs 25:6-7; 25:27; 27:2) to the teaching of Jesus (Matthew 20:20-28 and Luke 14:1-11). What are the lessons taught in each passage? How does true humility help stimulate us to serve others?

2. Read Mark 14:1-9 and 2 Timothy 1:16-18. How do these two passages demonstrate the attitudes taught in the previous question? What recognition did the woman and Onesiphorus receive? What can be learned from their example?

RESPOND ...

Principle: Serving others is one of the highest forms of serving God.

1. Identify one occasion when a person served and ministered to you or your family. What did they do? How did you feel? Did their example spur you on to serve others?

2. List three practical ways you can serve the members of your study group (or a group in which you participate). Evaluate the practicality of each form of service with the members of your group.

Spend time in prayer, asking God to give you the opportunity to put into practice what you have learned.

CHAPTER 9
UNITED WE STAND

Pastor Arturo Velasco called and wanted to come over for coffee. *Again? Didn't we meet twice last week?* There was a sense of urgency in his voice, though, and I knew he needed to talk. Aware it was neither the coffee nor the company he really desired, I invited him over to my house.

"You're not going to believe it, man!" He started on his tirade. "They're going to tear up our permit for the youth concert."

I listened as he explained in great detail his visit to the municipal office. Arturo faced injustice and veiled persecution as the local government official had threatened to cancel the permission for an evangelistic concert planned for the following week.

We spent the next couple of hours talking about the problem. We discussed various angles and strategies of how to deal with the obnoxious person in the permits office. We thought of a 'Plan B' which was later scrapped for 'Plan C.' We prayed and promised to spend time on our knees as we kept the situation before God.

When I dropped Arturo off at the church, he thanked me for my help. Something clicked as I realized what had transpired. I had not offered any great nuggets of truth nor insights he didn't already know. I didn't take away the problem. The coffee, although strong and flavorful, wasn't reason enough to pass a couple of hours together. What Arturo needed was someone with whom he could share his burden. He wanted someone to listen to the situation and tell him he wasn't crazy.

I need this kind of person in my life more often than I care to admit. I have a small group of friends or mentors from whom I seek help and counsel. They are men who are willing to sit down over a cup of strong cappuccino and hear me rant and rave for an hour. My problems or issues don't get resolved with the wave of a magic wand when I'm with them, but it helps me to know that someone has heard me and cares about the situation. It gives me a sense that I'm not going through things alone.

Barnabas and Paul knew the great strength in facing difficulties together. They ministered as a team in Antioch. Their missionary travels took them on a multi-city tour of Cyprus and eastern Asia Minor. They experienced great triumphs and faced difficult persecution. Their partnership spanned a number of years. Therefore, it is no surprise when the issues raised by the so-called "teachers of the circumcision" led the two men to tackle this problem together (Acts 15:1-4).

A Unifying Conflict?

Conflicts are usually seen as negative and disruptive. People can get caught up in the struggle between different positions. Groups tend to polarize around the leaders involved, taking sides and provoking heated discussion. Most conflicts result in unresolved problems.

The issue of Acts 15:1-4 needed to be addressed in a way that would lead to positive growth. The Church was forced to define its position as it considered the demands of those in favor of imposing Jewish laws and customs on all converts to Christianity. Paul and Barnabas were identified as legitimate and approved leaders of the group of believers. Together they presented a unified case against the demands of the Pharisees, serving as a highlight of the partnership they formed.

The immediate problem of Acts 15 revolved around the questions raised by Jewish Christians who were concerned with the practices of Gentile believers. The Jews, with years of experience in the faith, looked upon those who were younger in the faith and were not sure if they were actually saved. The deeper issue was to decide whether the Christian faith would be a revamped version of Jewish religion and customs, or whether it would be based upon Christ's forgiveness and transforming work.

The debate in Antioch did not resolve anything. Those visiting from Judea held to their unwavering position. Paul and Barnabas were opposed to their inflexible position, yet without the stamp of approval from the leadership in Jerusalem, were unable to reassure the onlookers from Antioch. An appeal was made to the only recognized body of leadership, the Jerusalem church.

There was potential for division and conflict as Paul and Barnabas tackled this question. To take sides with those who came from Judea could deeply hurt or even destroy the faith of the newer converts in Antioch. This could reap repercussions in the new groups of believers in Asia. To defend the cause of the Gentile believers without the backing of Church leadership would open a whole new set of problems, challenging its authority.

In their opening argument the leaders of the converted group of Pharisees stated: "The Gentiles must be circumcised and required to obey the law of Moses" (Acts 15:5). The cards were on the table and the debate had begun.

This conflict served to bring Paul and Barnabas together. As the representatives of the Antioch church to resolve this divisive question, the two men drew upon the strength of a united position.

Principles of Effective Problem Solving

The opposing groups had come to an impasse. They could not resolve their conflict on their own and appealed for mediation from an authoritative body to determine the answers to the questions at hand.

This step followed the pattern taught by Jesus, calling for the involvement of a mediator if two parties were unable to settle an issue on their own (Matthew 18:16). Instead of quibbling over who was right and who was wrong, the Antioch leadership took the wise step in seeking the counsel of authoritative and respected leaders.

The pattern Barnabas and Paul followed gives insights into an effective approach to resolving conflicts. They were not sent out as two lone sojourners to face what had the potential to be a hostile audience but were sent together with other members of the Antioch church (Acts 15:2). They asked for a clear and defined position from the apostles in Jerusalem. They showed wisdom in not confronting the situation alone.

Upon arriving in Jerusalem, both parties were given the opportunity to express their viewpoint. The group of Pharisees started with a demand for Gentile believers to comply with Mosaic law. Peter, sharing from his personal encounter with Cornelius (Acts 10), interjected and called for the Council to consider the question of salvation through the grace offered by the Lord (Acts 15:11). Barnabas and Paul were then called upon to share from their experience, following a protocol established by the Jerusalem leadership.[1] All involved had an opportunity to speak.

The order of some of the events leading up to the Council's decision is not clear. There may have been times of discussion, prayer, and fasting. James, the brother of Jesus, as the recognized leader of the Council, was given the final word. His decision reflected a compromise which allowed non-Jewish believers to be free of the cultural demands of the law. It dealt with the important issues of singular worship to God and holy living.

All present were in accord with the decision, and rejoiced in the edict. The later description that "it seemed good to the Holy Spirit and to us" (Acts 15:28) sums up the general acceptance of James' position. While the same problem would later surface, the issue was dealt with in a satisfactory manner. The declaration of the Council was put in writing and would be delivered to the groups of Gentile believers.

Identifying Threats to Unity

The letter sent as the report of the Jerusalem Council addressed various issues (Acts 15:22-29). It not only treated the immediate problem brought by those demanding a strict adherence to Jewish customs, but it identified other concerns. James and the leadership of the Church effectively defused potential bombs that could cause great disunity among the different groups who made up the Church.

Amazingly, the same basic controversies have plagued the Church throughout history. There is a need for leaders to help younger followers to identify these issues before they become larger-than-life problems. Threats to the unity and effectiveness of the Church need to be exposed, and the roots of potential problem addressed.

The opening statement of the letter sent by the Jerusalem leaders to the Gentile believers questioned the authority of the teachers who stirred up problems in Antioch. "We have heard that some went out from us without our authorization and disturbed you, troubling your minds with what they said" (Acts 15:24).

The members of the Antioch church, led by Barnabas and Paul, questioned the teaching that apparently came from Jerusalem. Their sharp disagreement with the content of what the members of the legalistic group were teaching caused them to appeal to the recognized authority of the early Church. With one simple statement, the Jerusalem Council distanced itself from those who disturbed the believers in Antioch. In doing so, faith in Jesus Christ was not a revamped form of Judaism, but indeed a revelation from God for a community that would be inclusive, not exclusive.

Many potential problems to the unity of a group of people can be avoided when there are clear authority structures. When the lines of responsibility are muddied by uncertain credentials or subtly different teachings, confusion settles in like a cloud. The first question to be addressed when a new or radically different teaching is presented is: By what authority are these doctrines being taught?

At times questions of interpretation come into our churches. These must be dealt with by giving a clear biblical answer. We need to allow for the possibility of differing opinions, but a clear foundation must be presented to defend the position of the church or group. It is for this reason doctrinal statements exist.

The specific problem of legalistic adherence to Jewish law was expressed in the demand for male converts to submit themselves to circumcision. This was partially rooted in a sense of superiority and pride. It was a result of focusing on the differences between the groups of believers, not on what they had in common. The obvious physical distinction caused Jewish believers to question the salvation of those who would not follow the letter of the law. Their faith was based on what they did, not in Whom they believed.

The early Church was dealing with issues that had never been addressed. The teaching of Jesus about following Jewish law had to be applied. The basic question was whether external practices or a transformed inner life constituted salvation. The answer to this question was to set the course for the inclusion of many future generations of believers.

Some would like to believe that today's Church is beyond placing importance on external or cultural practices to define Christianity? But is it?

Without entering into thorny doctrinal controversies, let me call attention to some issues raised within denominational groups. German Baptists, upon considering the tobacco farms of some of their American counterparts, shed real tears into their beer. Brazilian Pentecostals are scandalized by the loose practices of their Swedish founders who allow women to wear pants to public services. Colombian believers are shocked to learn that small group Bible studies in South Africa can have more than twelve members. Korean Christians, who struggle to keep their eyes open at the all-night prayer vigils common in South American churches, question the sincerity of their Latin American brothers who are unable to wake up for a 5:00 a.m. prayer service.

The examples listed are real. They all have one thing in common: a focus on external practices which have nothing to do with salvation. This tends to lead to a sense of unhealthy spiritual superiority.

The demand for Gentile believers to follow the observation of Old Testament law was the result of a focus on minor issues, not major questions of the faith. The observance of circumcision, an outward evidence or sign, was deemed more important than an inward obedience to the principles behind Old Testament law. Those who taught this doctrine did not understand the teachings of Jesus, and reverted to a legalistic observance of rituals and religious practices. There was little understanding of grace, forgiveness, or of God's plan to reach all people with the Gospel message.

The issues the apostles and the Jerusalem Council deemed as more important than circumcision are noteworthy. Gentile believers were urged not to eat meat that had been offered to idols, nor the flesh of a strangled or improperly bled-out animal. They were also asked to avoid sexual immorality. These cases had direct implications for the religious practices of the day and concerned themselves with holy living and separation from incorrect worship.

The eating of meat sacrificed to idols was considered to be an integral part of worship of the Greek gods. Paul would expand upon this issue in 1 Corinthians 8:1-13, teaching the importance of not knowingly entering into this practice. Christians were urged to distance themselves from these practices as a statement of allegiance to God.

Another example is the order to abstain from sexually immoral practices related to the pagan rituals, as well as to living a separated and holy life. Sexual intercourse was considered to be one of the highest forms of Greek worship. Temple prostitution, homosexuality, and other perversions were considered an important part of Greek religious life. The command to maintain a biblical pattern of sanctification in marriage and sexual behavior isolated Christians from the devastating results that these acts reaped upon the family structure.

The leaders in Jerusalem did not throw out all of the teachings of Jewish law and conduct. Their concern was to focus on the main issues of a life separated for worship of God and holy conduct. Many of the Jewish ritualistic practices and observations, together with their cultural implications, were not understood by Gentile believers and thus did not have deep significance. Baptism and the Lord's Supper were maintained as the two key elements of Christian practice because they were initiated and endorsed by Christ. What was deemed a priority by Church leaders was to live a life of worship to the true God and to offer their lives as a holy sacrifice as part of their high calling in Christ Jesus.

The minor issue of circumcision had the potential to divide and damage the young Church. Based on a strict observance of Jewish law, it was not a vital element of the teaching of Christ and was not included as a required observance by Church leaders. On the other hand, true worship and living a holy and separated life were deemed important elements of the expression of a true follower of Jesus Christ. The leaders focused on the major questions of the faith.

Have things really changed over the centuries? The Church continues to struggle through minor issues that can cloud or even eclipse major threats to true Christian doctrine. Smaller issues (such as worship styles or dress codes) threaten to divide churches. The squabbles over these areas receive our undivided attention, while issues that undermine the authority of the Scriptures or the conduct of members goes unchecked.

We have to step back and examine whether an issue is worthy of our attention and time. Is the color of the carpet more important than the temptations youth are facing? Does the length of the hair of a worship leader determine his or her spirituality? Does it matter to God if a brother or sister raises their hands or kneels quietly in the aisle as they praise Him?

Four godly men were sent to communicate the decision made in Jerusalem (Acts 15:22). Silas and Judas were respected leaders who verified the content of the decision, adding their moral authority. They stood with

Barnabas and Paul, who were commended for their allegiance to the cause of Christ. The presence of these men underlined the critical issue of Christ-like character as the basis for authoritative teaching.

It was not sufficient that a letter be sent. The churches affected by the questions dealt with at the Jerusalem Council would be visited by men who lived out and understood the truth they presented. Unlike an edict passed on by some unknown authority, the Antioch church received notice of the decision from representatives elected to encourage and deliver the decision. The people who received these men were glad and encouraged (Acts 15:31). Instead of an order coming down from leaders in Jerusalem, the divisive question ended up as an opportunity for ministry and growth.

The integrity and character of Paul and Barnabas, as well as of those sent from Jerusalem, was undeniable. They were recognized as true men of God in whom moral authority rested. When they spoke, people listened. Their words were not their own, but were considered to be the very words of God.

I know a few people who have this special gift. Their words can defuse a problem and bring issues into focus in a short time. The weight of God's approval upon their lives is evident as they speak. They usually don't talk in harsh or condemning tones, but rather address the main issues with few words. They have a unique gift of wisdom and are able to bring people together. When problems arise, I seek them for counsel.

The promise of James 1:5 is: "If any of you lacks wisdom, you should ask God, who gives generously to all without finding fault, and it will be given to you." My experience is that the wisdom of God will come to me through a number of sources. It can come through the study of the Scriptures. It can come through truth shared in a book. However, more often than in any other form, God's wisdom comes through seeking the counsel of godly men and women.

Finally, the letter sent by the apostles highlights the need for convergence of opinion. This can only be brought by the unifying work of the Holy Spirit. The words "It seemed good to the Holy Spirit and to us" crown the correspondence with a seal of divine approval. It provided a declaration of unity and an example for all believers to follow.

The Holy Spirit unifies and rallies believers around the banner of Christ. When the Spirit is present, there can be agreement even in the face of diverse opinions. When the Spirit is present, Christ's deep desire is accomplished: that His followers be one just as He is one with His Father (John 17:21). As Christians experience this reality, the world will believe that Jesus was sent by God (John 17:21). It is also for this reason that Christ's followers are to strive to preserve the unity of the Spirit (Ephesians 4:3).

It is most unfortunate when some use their particular beliefs regarding the work of the Holy Spirit to justify and promote division. A focus on minor issues, such as worship styles or practices, cannot be justified as works of the Spirit. I know of some leaders who hide their disapproval or jealousy behind such differences. This should not be the case.

One of the benefits I have experienced as I've lived in various countries and cultures is to see the principle of the unity of the Spirit in daily situations. Language and cultural barriers do not weigh upon me when I know the person I am dealing with loves and serves the same heavenly Father. Differences in our appearance have little to do with a heart set on following God. I may not understand the language of a person who is praying for me, but I can sense the love and passion he or she has for God. There is a bond of unity which surpasses all of these factors when we are part of the same spiritual family.

The convergence of opinion experienced in the Jerusalem Council was beautiful. There is no doubt that those involved spent much time in prayer, seeking God's will in this situation. There was a sharing of God's work in the lives and experiences of the many Gentile believers. The expressions of mutual respect and unity served to strengthen each participant in their faith. It was a true work of the Spirit to bring believers together, united under the banner of Jesus.

Why do we not see more expressions of unity of the Spirit? Perhaps we get caught up in some of the same issues that began to strangle the growth of the early Church. Questions of the authority of a teacher or their teachings go unchecked. A focus on external practices as opposed to inner transformation is permitted. We major on the minor issues and lose sight of truly worshipping God and living a life worthy of His name. We seek wisdom from the latest gurus without knowing them to be people of God. We even mistake spiritual maturity as something that can cause division and strife among fellow believers. It's time to heed the lessons learned from the letter written at the first council of leaders in Jerusalem.

If you are going to deal with people, you have to learn to resolve conflicts. If you are going to disciple a group of people, they will observe you and learn from you as you face personal differences or disturbing questions. This is inevitable.

It is helpful to recognize potential problems and deal with them before they start. It is equally important to know and understand the proper biblical procedure for encountering issues. The Scriptures do not gloss over conflict, but rather present a true-to-life perspective which enables us to know how to deal with troubling situations.

The process of conflict resolution was the final lesson Barnabas shared with his disciple. He and Paul had walked many miles together on their mission to share the Gospel. They had experienced the damp walls of jail cells, faced fierce persecution, and encountered hostile audiences. They had seen people restored through a new covenant relationship with Christ, churches established, and many wonderful signs of God's power.

It seems ironic that the lessons learned in the successful resolution of the Jerusalem Council could not be applied to the personal disagreement Barnabas and Paul would face upon returning to Antioch when they found themselves in another conflict. However, in this case they would not have the same happy ending.

Study Guide

ACTIVE LEARNING ...

Form groups of two or three. Take on the role of Sherlock Holmes and Dr. Watson to complete the following exercises. Be prepared to share your findings with the larger group.

1. List five of your all-time favorite dynamic duos (secular or biblical, real or imaginary). What did each of the partnerships you listed accomplish? What characterized their ability to face difficult situations?

2. Identify three characteristics which enable teams to face and resolve conflict. What are the similarities with the example of Paul and Barnabas in Acts 15?

CONSIDER ...

Read each passage and answer the following questions:

1. In Deuteronomy 1:19-40, what problem did Joshua and Caleb face? What does this passage teach about their character and belief in God? What was the result of their standing together?

2. Describe the conflict Daniel and his friends faced in Daniel 1:1-20? How were they able to resolve the situation? What does their example teach us?

3. What were the circumstances leading to Peter and John's audience before the Sanhedrin in Acts 4:1-22? How would you describe the defense of their cause? What were the benefits of facing this situation together?

RESPOND ...

Principle: "Though one may be overpowered, two can defend themselves. A cord of three strands is not quickly broken." (Ecclesiastes 4:12)

1. Read Ecclesiastes 4:9-12. Write out this passage, personalizing each verse with the pronouns, I, we, and us. Include the names of those you consider your helpers and mentors.

2. Spend time thanking God for these people. Write a brief note expressing your gratitude for their support.

CHAPTER 10
AGREE TO DISAGREE

I sat and listened as my colleagues expressed their feelings. "If you're willing to accept three conditions, then go ahead with your plans," they said.

"I wouldn't have it any other way," I said, without blinking an eye. I didn't want to concede they might be right. There was too much at stake. A stalemate was the best I could hope for at this point.

Our missionary team had come to a conclusion about the timing and method of starting a third church in Porto Alegre. We were in full agreement that planting another church was a part of our vision and goals, but we had different ideas about when this should take place. We were all convinced of using home Bible study groups to begin to infiltrate a new area of the city, but were unsure if we were prepared for the task. As we came to our decision there were many unanswered questions.

I was eager to press on and begin something new, taking advantage of an opportunity set before us. Together we had prayed and sought God's will. I thought I was rather eloquent when I challenged our missionary team to "seize the day" and to consider this "open door" as from the Lord. The words of my high school drafting teacher once again described my method of dealing with challenges: "You rush in where angels fear to tread."

My older and wiser colleagues had other ideas. They expressed their desire to strengthen the two existing works in the city, mentoring the leaders who had recently been installed. We would be short-staffed with the departure of two couples who were scheduled for a year of deputation in North America. They reminded me of my responsibilities with the newly formed Leadership Training School, a modular form of ministerial preparation. They agreed we had a great opportunity before us, but were not as confident that the time was right for beginning a new project.

We arrived at a compromise which included three important aspects. I would be allowed to start the new home Bible study, provided I did not relinquish any of my responsibilities at the Leadership Training School. Second, the new initiative would not be considered or referred to as a church planting project, which meant it would not receive any mission funding. Third, I could only proceed with the group if I would do my part in the mentorship program we had established for leaders of the existing churches. Under these conditions I was given a "green light" to go ahead.

I wasn't about to let this opportunity slip by. Our team had spent hours working through this decision and now there was a crack in the door of opportunity. I wanted to take advantage of it. *Carpe Diem!*

A Divinely Appointed Disagreement?

We previously spoke of how God sovereignly arranges for meetings between those who do not know Christ and those who do. These divine appointments are *kairos* moments when God brings people and circumstances together to accomplish His eternal purposes, leading to the conversion of an individual.[1]

I wonder about whether God might use other circumstances to do His will. Could it be that there is such a thing as a divine disagreement? Would God use something as unspiritual as an argument to further His kingdom or to direct individuals?

If you have never worked through a conflict with a trusted friend or a respected leader you probably will not understand or appreciate Luke's description of the disagreement between Barnabas and Paul (Acts 15:36-41). You will probably struggle with their conclusions and question their spirituality as they each staunchly defended their positions. You may ask yourself how two people involved in the work of the Kingdom of God could allow an insignificant issue to come between them? But it happens more often than you may think.

Barnabas and Paul had recently returned from the Jerusalem Council, amplifying the questions raised in trying to understand their argument. They had weathered the storm of criticism and uncertainty over the issues that concerned Gentile believers. Their sense of partnership was at a high point. However, this new crisis would test their unity and friendship. It would cause them to go their separate ways and would mark the end of one of the most outstanding ministry partnerships in the Scriptures.

As with any relationship that goes beyond a surface level, Barnabas and Paul found themselves in the midst of situations in which they did not agree. While only two of their disagreements are recorded in the pages of the Bible, others likely took place.[2]

The two disagreed over the inclusion of Mark on their second missionary journey (Acts 15:36-41). When they decided to visit the new groups of believers, delivering the decision of the Jerusalem Council, Barnabas wanted to take his nephew, Mark, also known as John; Paul did not. In the end they agreed to disagree and each of them went their separate way, visiting different cities.

Barnabas saw beyond his nephew's earlier disappointments and failure, seeing potential in his life. On the other hand, Paul rejected Mark on the basis of his poor track record. Paul reminded Barnabas that Mark had abandoned them on their first missionary voyage, returning home in the middle of the journey.

Allow me a little creativity as I imagine the conversation between the two early Church leaders:

"That 'mama's boy' deserted us just when things got interesting! He's immature and unreliable! He couldn't take the heat then and he's no different now," says Paul.

"But you can't give up on him," Barnabas protests. "He's learned from his mistakes. You can't just throw in the towel without giving him a second chance."

"He'll be back in Jerusalem before you know it," states Paul, a disgusted look on his face. "If he wasn't a relative, I know you'd see it my way. You've got to stop putting family ahead of ministry."

"That's not fair," says Barnabas, pointing an accusing finger at Paul. "If you could only get over the incident in Pamphylia, you'd see him as a potentially productive member of our team."

"I don't think so." Paul shrugs as he turns his back and starts to walk away.

"What if that was the way we acted when..." Barnabas stops before completing his question. Paul is already out of hearing distance. Barnabas decides not to yell, but in his mind he starts to formulate "Plan B."

To say Barnabas or Paul was right in this conflict is presumptuous. Each man took on a part of the task of visiting the new believers in the cities where they had preached. Barnabas chose to return to Cyprus, his native land. He took Mark, who had been present on the first leg of the inaugural missionary journey. Paul included Silas as his new partner, a young leader who displayed great potential. By reaching a compromise, the two men multiplied their work and effectiveness.

If we desire to be used by God to impact the lives of others, we have to learn to resolve conflicts. We might be in the middle of the problem or act as an outside observer, but we will be asked to deal with differences of opinion, philosophy, and personalities. If not handled wisely, these conflicts can rob us of our energy and joy in serving God, leading to disillusionment, comparisons, and even despair. Many people have been shipwrecked as they failed to resolve issues with others.

While disagreements are an unavoidable part of working and dealing with people, they do not have to crush or defeat us. They can lead to positive growth, especially when compared to the consequences that result when they are suppressed or left unresolved. Those who give in to the temptation to avoid them altogether soon find themselves entangled in deeper, more complicated problems. Those who face and resolve their conflicts can go on to act as peacemakers who help others deal with tough relational issues. Learning to deal with differences is an arduous task that takes time and energy, but it equips us to face the challenges of life and ministry.

We can learn from the conflict between Barnabas and Paul because their parting of ways lent itself to positive growth. We may even concede that in God's sovereign grace this was a divinely appointed disagreement. Consider three great lessons to be learned from this event:

1. Know the time to release a learner.
2. Focus on giftedness and calling.
3. Trust in God's sovereignty to lead and guide.

Know the Time to Release a Learner

There comes a time when a mentor or teacher must send out his or her disciples and allow them to put into practice what they have learned. Practical experience fine-tunes what the disciples learned in a classroom or see in the lives of others. Jesus did this on a number of occasions with His disciples.

The disagreement between Paul and Barnabas served to open new doors. They parted company with the common goal to advance the Kingdom of God, but their plans for completing the task differed. Paul preached in new cities and broke ground for taking the Gospel to Europe. Barnabas went on to encourage and build up existing groups of believers.

The time had come for Paul to take on an apprentice, and parting ways with Barnabas gave him freedom to develop his ministry in new ways. Something deep in Paul's spirit was moving him to take these steps. It was directly related to his calling and passion to preach the Gospel to those who had not heard.

The timing of the Jerusalem Council is an issue to be considered. Paul was no longer seen as a renegade by the leadership of the Church. He was now a trusted messenger of the Gospel. His ministry with Barnabas served as a time of testing, and resulted in his approval and acceptance. The validity of Paul's ministry no longer hinged upon Barnabas' stellar reputation.

Barnabas could see Paul's ministry taking on a new focus. During their first journey, Barnabas had the wisdom to promote Paul as the main spokesperson of their missionary team. He saw leadership characteristics in Paul. He knew a time would come for Paul to develop his own ministry.

Just how one goes about the task of releasing a disciple varies with each situation. Sometimes God allows circumstances that force two people to part through a move to a different city or ministry. At times, issues like philosophy of ministry or vision are involved. There are instances when the people involved feel good about the parting of ways, and sometimes they struggle with the decision. There is a great need for wisdom, humility, and reliance upon God when approaching this subject.

Focus on Giftedness and Calling

The parting of Barnabas and Paul allowed each person to focus on his giftedness and calling. Whether they recognized this at the time, we are not sure.

Barnabas, from the moment he is introduced in Acts Chapter 4, is known as the "son of encouragement." His name says it all. He was not a prophet who stood and cried out to the bystanders. He was the one who came to a fallen or needy brother, put his arm around his shoulder, and lifted him up. This is who God created him to be.

An apostolic and evangelistic calling upon Paul's life is revealed in a number of biblical passages. In Acts 9:15 God told Ananias "This man is my chosen instrument to proclaim my name to the Gentiles and their kings and to the people of Israel." "It has always been my ambition to preach the gospel where Christ was not known, so that I would not be building on someone else's foundation," said Paul in Romans 15:20. From the moment of his conversion, Paul was called to preach to the unconverted.

The two men did things differently from each other. Barnabas couldn't insist that Paul fit into his mold. It was equally unfitting for Paul to demand that Barnabas be more like him.

When we come to understand who we are and accept the way God wants to use us in the Kingdom, we are able to experience rest and peace in our ministry. God uses others in different ways. This allows us to focus on what we are called to do, rather than striving to be someone we are not. As stated previously, this involves accepting who we are and not seeing others as a threat or competition in ministry. This requires that we know the areas in which God has gifted us and focus on ministries congruent to our calling. It also includes partnering with those who complement our giftedness to ensure a fuller, more well-rounded ministry.[3]

George Barna, in his book *The Power of Vision*, speaks of the "60/40 Principle of Spiritual Giftedness."[4] He teaches the need for individuals to be involved in ministries where at least 60 percent of their time is spent in activities matching their spiritual gifts. He teaches that fulfillment and a sense of divine direction are the experience of those ministering in areas of their giftedness. On the contrary, those who find themselves in roles that do not coincide with who God made them to be will be frustrated and unsettled. Although it is unlikely for a person to be involved in areas of their spiritual gifts all the time, a worthy goal for those in ministry is to seek a balance. They should be aware of the need to spend as much time as possible in ministries which correspond to their God-imparted giftedness.

There needs to be a strong commitment to discover and develop the spiritual gifts of those with whom we work. Otherwise we run the risk of difficulties and unnecessary tensions, whether they be over philosophy of ministry, goals, or practices. We may even find ourselves in a heated disagreement leading to a reordering of our ministry roles and teams.

This was the case in the disagreement between Barnabas and Paul. It caused each man to focus on his area of giftedness. The remaining chapters of the book of Acts and Paul's letters to the early churches are a testimony of the ministry God had prepared for him. The restoration of Mark serves as an example of the ongoing ministry exercised by Barnabas. The disagreement led to both men ministering out of their spiritual giftedness.

Trust in God's Sovereignty to Lead and Guide

Emotions must have been heavy as the two former partners in ministry, Barnabas and Paul, parted company. If the order of events in Acts 15:39 is correct, Barnabas departed with Mark for Cyprus. Paul soon followed with Silas, setting out for Syria and Cilicia. Both teams were commended by the church in Antioch and sent off with its blessing.

The rest of the book of Acts records the steps of Paul. Timothy was added to the team and became Paul's faithful coworker. Their relationship yielded another great example of mentorship. Paul followed his calling and took the gospel to Macedonia and other parts of the Roman world. The end of Barnabas and Paul's ministry relationship signaled the beginning of new ministries for Paul.

What happened to Barnabas and Mark? The extent of their visit to Cyprus and time together as a ministry team is not recorded in the Scriptures. Church history gives only a glimpse of further events in their lives. Although Barnabas did not slip into obscurity, he stepped out of the spotlight of the Scriptures. [5]

God's purposes were accomplished through the parting of Barnabas and Paul. God wanted Paul to be a vessel of blessing as he preached the gospel to the Gentile nations. God desired to see the restoration of Mark, who became the author of the gospel that bears his name. What at first glance seemed to be a difficult and distressing circumstance, in God's timing and direction, was a "win-win situation." It was God's sovereignty at work.

Disagreements are never an end in themselves, and are the opposite of qualities God wants to build into a believer's life. Peace is a fruit of the Spirit which should mark the life of a Christian (Galatians 5:22). Ephesians 4:3 contains a strong admonition to "Make every effort to keep the unity of the Spirit through the bond of peace." Speaking of the potential conflict between an unbelieving spouse with a partner who is a believer, Paul taught that "God has called us to live in peace" (1 Corinthians 7:15). Paul also reminded Timothy to live a peaceful and quiet life, clothed in godliness and holiness (1 Timothy 2:2). The Bible gives no basis to provoke conflict, but rather speaks of the need to work at ensuring peaceful relationships as the mark of the Christian life.

When conflicts arise, we need to be prepared to resolve and deal with them. They cannot be ignored. The danger they pose to the work of God and unity of the Church is serious. Like Barnabas and Paul, they may be used by God to teach lessons which can only be learned by agreeing to disagree on some issues.

I referred to the situation in Porto Alegre at the beginning of this chapter. It did not result in a disintegration of our ministry team. We struggled through the important issues of philosophy of ministry and goals. We heard each person's point of view, their dreams, and their sense of God's will and timing in the planting of another church. We had to consider strategy, as well as who would best fit into the church-planting situation. What was the outcome?

Looking back, I can understand my colleagues' caution at rushing into a new work. Our final year of ministry in Brazil was a blur of activity, and only a handful of the people who started the home Bible study stayed in the group. We could have devoted our time and energy to mentor other men and women who were more qualified to take on the task. At times I wondered whether we missed God's direction in this process.

But God showed His sovereign ways and surprised us all. Today there is a third church in a neighboring city. Our first feeble steps to start a new work inspired others to take up the challenge and to begin other studies. We didn't know it at the time, but God worked in spite of our differences of opinion to further His kingdom.

When we state that God is sovereign, we acknowledge that all events of our lives are under His watchful care. There is nothing which catches Him by surprise, and nothing He cannot use for His glory. We may not understand His purposes in what we perceive as His will, but we need to learn to trust Him as the One who orders the events of our lives.

Was either Barnabas or Paul "right" when they parted company? At the time they both defended their position. They would not have had such a sharp argument if they did not feel their case was worth making and the other was wrong. However, it does not matter who was "right." God worked through a human disagreement to accomplish His purposes.

Paul showed an apparent change of heart when years later he asked Timothy to "get Mark...because he is helpful to me in my ministry" (2 Timothy 4:11). Barnabas affirmed Mark's usefulness on the day he and Paul parted company.

Just like Paul, Mark would spend time watching and learning from Barnabas. As a result, the Mark of 2 Timothy 4:11 is a different person from who he was on the first missionary journey. The "Barnabas Factor" had reaped its positive effects again.

Study Guide

ACTIVE LEARNING ...

In small groups (or as an individual), prepare a eulogy which describes the end of the ministry relationship between Barnabas and Saul. What are four outstanding aspects you would highlight of their time together? How would you describe the circumstances leading to the end of their relationship? Share your descriptions with the rest of the group.

CONSIDER ...

1. Read the following passages. Briefly describe the parting of ways between the people involved. What are some of the positive lessons to be learned from each story? Are there elements which should be avoided?

    Moses and Joshua
    Deuteronomy 31:1-13; 34:1-9; and Joshua 1:1-9.

    David and Jonathan
    1 Samuel 20:1-42 and 2 Samuel 9:1-13.

    Jesus and his disciples
    Mark 14:12-26; John 14:1-14; 17:6-19; Matt. 28:16-20

    Barnabas and Paul
    Acts 15:36-41; Galatians 2:11-16; and 2 Timothy 4:11.

2. This chapter refers to three lessons which can be learned from the disagreement between Barnabas and Paul. What are the lessons to be learned? How do they apply to us today?

3. Reflect on a previous mentoring relationship you have had with another person. What were the means or circumstances used to bring an end or a new phase to this relationship? Share your experiences with your group.

RESPOND ...

Principle: God is not limited nor is He unable to work through situations when two people come to the point of "agreeing to disagree" over a dispute.

1. What can be done during a mentorship or team relationship to ensure a good ending and the continuation of effective ministry?

2. Reflect on the lessons learned in this chapter. What steps should be taken if a disagreement arises?

3. How can a proper understanding of spiritual gifts help deal with differences of opinion which can divide two people in a ministry team situation?

CHAPTER 11
WHICH WAY DID HE GO?

I hate high school reunions, even though I've never attended one. I shudder at the thought of rubbing shoulders with wrinkle-faced people who used to be my pimple-faced friends. I made sure that I had a good excuse not to appear at the 25th anniversary of my high school graduating class. Let me explain my position.

First, there would have been the embarrassing questions. Do you remember the time you dribbled grape soda down your white T-shirt while attempting to ask Sussie Sweetface on a date? Were you ever able to get beyond the words *parlez vous français*? Did you ever recover from the ridicule of vomiting in the middle of your tenth grade English exam? Weren't you the one who ripped a hole in your shorts when attempting the splits in gym class?

Second, there would be the two or three people who use these events to flaunt their success, or their latest plastic surgery. Like someone directly out of an infomercial, they are not present to meet people, but rather to be met. They just happen to let it be known that they're driving a BMW and receive a call on their cell phone about a major deal in Europe. Their tight stomach muscles and full head of hair would stand out like a famous chef eating at a cheap taco stand. They really don't seem to fit in.

Third, there would be the incredible stories of those who were not present. Did you hear about so-and-so? The only thing he ever manufactured was license plates. The girl who dated everyone is now working on her third marriage and fourth kid. The star quarterback never got beyond sandlot stardom and now sells used cars in a small town in the middle of nowhere. The brilliant girl who sat in front of you in English class—yes, the one you threw up on—suffered a nervous breakdown and is locked in a rubber room in a research facility.

Finally, there would be the now-retired teachers converging like vultures at a roadside picnic. They confirm their greatest suspicions which, according to them, were well-founded. They gather around the punch bowl, glaring at the crowd, waiting for a chance to pounce on a victim. Their tongues have sharpened with years of practicing their trade in smoky teachers' lounges. They all look exactly as they did twenty-some years ago. If you look closely enough, you'd see your history teacher is wearing the same tattered, tweed jacket.

So, you ask me why I avoid high school reunions like the plague? I think it's obvious. The comparisons, the awkward questions, the showoffs, and the attempts to relive a not-so-fabulous past are all reason enough for me. Why would anyone in their right mind submit themselves to such suffering?

I know there are some who do not share my point of view. Some get excited about meeting old friends, sharing a laugh, and getting reacquainted. They want to know where everyone is living and what they are doing. They look forward to meeting the aging teachers who inflicted arduous homework and administered tough exams. I have to admit I don't understand this breed of people, but they do exist.

I wonder if Barnabas ever showed up at a reunion of Jerusalem High? Did he ever get the chance to meet Paul and "chew the fat" or compare notes about Mark? Was he given the chance to tell his side of the story about the time he and Peter were swayed by the hypocritical gang out of Jerusalem? How would he explain his disappearing off the face of the earth? Or maybe Barnabas was like me, and none of this really mattered to him.

The Voice of History

Acts 15:39 is Luke's last reference to Barnabas. The pages of the Bible are strangely quiet after this point, with four fleeting mentions of his name. He joins a group of Paul's other colleagues who are referred to at specific periods in time, but who seem to vanish into thin air.

Church history gives some insights into the final stages of the life of Barnabas. Most references date to the late third and early fourth centuries. Eusebius, the recognized "Father of Church History," is one of many authors who wrote about Barnabas. Eusebius considered Barnabas as the "Fifteenth Apostle", an important figure in the spread of the Gospel to the Gentile world.[1]

Barnabas made various trips to his homeland, Cyprus. Acts 15:39 refers to his second voyage to Cyprus, most likely setting sail for the island's eastern city of Salamis from the port of Seleucia. Barnabas and Mark revisited the groups that were established during the previous missionary journey. They founded a church that has withstood the tests of time, including an invasion of the Muslims in the mid-seventh century.[2] To this day Cypriot Orthodox Christianity reveres and honors the man they consider their patriarchal founder.

Barnabas' inclusion of Mark would later be vindicated by Paul's recognition of the spiritual growth which had taken place in the life of the younger leader (2 Timothy 4:11). It is unclear how much time Mark spent with Barnabas. The two were united years later in Salamis when Barnabas suffered his martyrdom.[3] What is clear is that Mark's restoration was a direct result of Barnabas' influence and patience.

Tradition says that Barnabas visited various cities. Like Paul, Barnabas earned his living as he continued to minister and encourage churches (1 Corinthians 9:5-6). This enabled him to travel and not be a burden to the new congregations. Catholic historians consider it probable that Barnabas traveled to Alexandria and was among the earliest of the apostles to preach on African soil. He is also mentioned as having ministered in Rome and Milan, adding two important stopovers to his itinerary.[4]

A special relationship between Barnabas and Christians of the city of Alexandria adds credence to his possible travels to Egypt. While Eusebius credits Mark as the founder of the Coptic Church, Barnabas visited and taught in Alexandria on a number of occasions.[5] The apocryphal Epistle of Barnabas, believed to have been written in Alexandria (130 A.D.), drew upon the knowledge of Barnabas' visits to the Egyptian city to add authenticity to this record.[6]

The Church of England also considers Barnabas to be an important historical figure in their development. English historians of the 12th Century record a verbal record of Barnabas and Aristobulus visiting British shores.

They apparently focused their ministry in Glastonbury, the birthplace of Anglo-Saxon Christianity. To this day the strong link between Britain and the apostle from Cyprus is seen in the frequent use of "Saint Barnabas" as a name for Anglican and Episcopalian perishes.[7]

Fox's Book of Martyrs considers the death of Barnabas in A.D. 73 to be a part of the first general persecution under Nero.[8] Legend asserts he was stoned to death in Salamis, a port city on the island of Cyprus. Mark was present and placed a scroll of Matthew's Gospel on the fallen apostle. Not all of these details are verifiable, as some of the historical evidence is derived from the extra-biblical letter of *The Acts of Barnabas*.[9]

A resounding theme surfaces as historians relate the actions of Barnabas. Barnabas was not a man who sat and watched the world pass by. As he slipped out of the limelight of the Scriptures, he continued to faithfully serve God. He preached the name of Christ, taking the Gospel to three continents. Barnabas did not "disappear off the face of the earth," but rather he quietly imparted his life to others who would in turn impact their world.

The lesson learned from the voice of history is one of dedicated service to God. Barnabas' influence, investing his life in the life of a few faithful men, reached to many corners of the globe.

This lesson remains true for today. At any given moment there are Christians who are faithfully but quietly serving God. They may not have great fame nor hold official positions, but they make a difference in the world. Like Barnabas, they work out their faith in practical ways and reach people with the love and encouragement of God.

The Hall of Fame of the Unnoticed

Hebrews 11 is known as "The Hall of Fame of Faith." Its author traces the work of God in the lives of faithful men and women of the Old Testament. This "great cloud of witnesses" encourages Christians of all times to live their lives in the same manner, faithfully serving God (Hebrews 12:1).

A group of unnamed people are mentioned in the famous "faith chapter." The women received back their dead, others were tortured, and some who faced jeers and floggings are unidentified. Those who were stoned, cut in two, or wandered about in sheepskins remain anonymous.

Hebrews 11:38 comments that "the world was not worthy of them," yet they are commended for their faith.

I believe Barnabas was an unsung hero who fits into this category. He joins others who slipped in and out of the pages of biblical history with little fanfare. He didn't stand out as a great evangelist or pastor of a large mega-church, but he serves as an example of an ordinary person God used to build His extraordinary kingdom.

If there were a "Hall of Fame of the Unnoticed," Barnabas would be among the first candidates to be considered. "He was a good man, full of the Holy Spirit and faith" would be the caption placed under his portrait. Photos of his disciples, together with a brief description of their relationship, would line one side of the "Barnabas corner." A small map and a tribute from the churches he helped establish would complete the display area. Visitors who pass by too quickly without taking a second look would miss out on a great discovery.

The history of the Christian faith is filled with men and women who fit this description. They come under the "others" category of Hebrews 11. They are the men and women who gave their lives for others, expressing God's love and character in tangible ways. Some were only appreciated after their deaths. Others go unnoticed on earth, awaiting their reward from the One who recognizes all they did and said. They form part of the "great cloud of witnesses" who have impacted the world for God's eternal Kingdom.

I have a few candidates of my own. Various people mentioned in previous chapters of this book would be part of the list of names I would submit. There would be a number of Sunday School teachers, boys club leaders, and others who influenced my life who would get my vote. My grandmother, a tiny German *Oma* who prayed that two of her 43 grandchildren would enter the ministry, would make my list. I would nominate Ken Shauer, who gave his time, home, van, and life for the young people in our first youth group. Seu Edu, an elderly African-Brazilian man who adopted and prayed for my children as if they were his own grandchildren, would also be part of my personal "Hebrews 11" list.

I feel the same constraints as the author of Hebrews when I say there isn't room or time to tell of all of the people who could be inducted into this hall of fame. They are ordinary men and women who faithfully serve God and touch the lives of others. They may not have conquered nations or built architectural wonders, but they have edified and encouraged people. While their work and impact on earth may go unnoticed by the crowds, they are not overlooked by God. Their work is also never forgotten by those who have been impacted and transformed through contact with these godly saints. They leave a legacy which forms a "great cloud of witnesses" to encourage future generations to follow their example.

A Lasting Legacy

Barnabas' impact can be measured by the transformed lives of his disciples. His ministry hinged upon touching individuals who would go on to reach others. What mattered to Barnabas was to leave a lasting legacy that would be carried on by the generations to come.

The New Testament gives no better example of a godly encourager. Barnabas not only stood up for Paul, but he also gave Mark a second chance. No one knows how many individuals benefited from this unique ministry over the course of time. Barnabas, known as the "son of encouragement," lived up to his name.

Barnabas' disciples left a literary legacy, as Christians of all generations are indebted to Paul and Mark for their contributions to the New Testament. Mark's Gospel is considered to be the first of the written accounts of the life of Jesus. Paul was a prolific writer, developing a ministry of the written word as he counseled churches and individuals. The two men, enriched and encouraged during their time of mentorship under Barnabas, surfaced as God's chosen instruments to transmit His eternal message.

Barnabas may have directly influenced his disciple's writing careers. Tertullian, an early Church father, attributed the book of Hebrews to Barnabas.[10] Often considered a part of Pauline literature, any stylistic resemblance between the book of Hebrews and Paul's letters could be explained by understanding that a disciple becomes like his mentor. Barnabas, who was a Levite, also had a rich understanding of Jewish culture and customs. While there are other strong arguments in favor of Paul's authorship, the anonymous nature of the book of Hebrews remains an unsolved mystery.

The undeniable multiplying effect of Barnabas' life and ministry upon others is the outstanding factor that made him a man of impact. Barnabas' investment in the lives of Paul and Mark reaped a harvest which reached far beyond his travels. His ability to see potential in the lives of others was a gift from God. To this day it is recognized that Barnabas left a lasting legacy.

I learned a valuable lesson from my first mentor in full-time ministry. Pastor Dallas Strangway had years of experience and was willing to share his nuggets of wisdom with me. He helped me understand when and where to measure success or failure as a pastor.

At the time, I was frustrated because I didn't feel my ministry was fruitful. I compared myself to the pastor who had previously held my post, focusing on his evangelistic abilities. In my years as a youth pastor I didn't feel I had had many teens come to faith in Christ. Numbers hadn't been bad, but I definitely didn't see the explosive growth that I expected of myself.

"Don't measure yourself against others," said Pastor Strangway. "Don't measure results now, but rather in three or four years. The fruit that remains is what really counts."

These timely words of counsel helped me to move on to a new ministry setting. They encouraged me to pray for those into whom I invested my life. I was a discipler and was able to help those who had accepted Christ in my predecessor's ministry. My mentor's words also enabled me to remember the importance of being the right person before doing the right things. No longer did I focus on numerical results, but considered that which would produce a lasting legacy.

Rhonda and I maintain contact with this church. Every time we go back we're impacted by those who come to talk to us. They are no longer teens, but are the leaders of their church. They are Sunday school teachers and youth sponsors who are making their impact upon the lives of others. They barely resemble the freckle-faced teens who were a part of our youth group.

"Do you remember me? I was that obnoxious kid who always asked irrelevant questions at Bible Study?"

"Do you recall the time I sneaked out of the cabin and went for a midnight swim with my girlfriend? You really bawled me out for that one!"

"Remember the time we went fishing and you fell in the river? We laughed so hard we thought we were going to burst. And we laughed and watched as you got angry!"

"Did you ever think I'd turn out OK?"

There were times during our years of ministry in that place when Rhonda and I didn't think the teens were paying attention. There were days we felt like giving up and throwing in the towel. Often we were driven to our knees in prayer for the needs of our kids, desiring to see God's work accomplished in their lives.

We are thankful that God used us in the lives of these young people. Today they are adults serving Him in their local churches. Some have moved to different cities, and are involved in their churches. We're amazed at how He used our lives to love and make an impact upon the lives of a group of teenagers.

Some of our teens are not following or serving God. Our hearts ache for those who are "shipwrecked in their faith." We pray that someone else will come alongside them to draw them back to Christ.

Changed lives are the currency of heaven. The example of Barnabas teaches that there is only one inheritance worth leaving behind: the transformed lives of people. A good name is golden, but lives that go on to serve God and faithfully share the love of Christ reap an eternal harvest.

As I write and reflect I am struck by the need for men and women who will be like Barnabas. God gives some people a ministry which resembles that of the Apostle Paul, but they are not in the majority. Much of heaven's work is accomplished through people who are not spiritual giants, but rather are faithful men and women who understand what it means to serve God and others. They leave a lasting legacy, changing the world one life at a time.

I am also moved to give thanks for the many who have been "Barnabas" for me. God used men and women to guide me in my spiritual growth and encouraging me along the path. I shudder to think where I would be today if they had not come into my life.

Finally, I am challenged to make my impact in the lives of others. I don't need recognition or fanfare to do so, but rather the conviction that God wants to use me to touch the lives of others. The presence of the Holy Spirit, who lived in Barnabas and lives in me, enables me to be a person God can use to accomplish His purposes. As I surrender myself to His leading, God will use me as an instrument in the lives of others.

Study Guide

ACTIVE LEARNING ...

Make a list of nominees to the Hall of Fame of the Unnoticed. Include five biblical characters and five personal examples of people who have quietly been used by God to impact the world. Answer the following questions before bringing your list of nominees to the larger group.

1. Are there similarities between your candidates? What characteristics mark these people as nominees for this honor?

2. If possible, identify the process or circumstances which produced these character qualities in their lives.

CONSIDER ...

One characteristic of a person who leaves a lasting inheritance is their faithfulness. Carefully read the following passages and answer the questions which relate to this quality.

1. In 1 Kings 2:1-2, what was David's main concern as he handed the kingdom of Israel to his son? How did Solomon react? What was the legacy David left behind?

2. Compare 1 Samuel 26:21 with Acts 13:22. List the character qualities of David and Saul, noting the results for which they are remembered. What elements led to Saul's moral failure? How did David develop "a heart after God?"

3. In 2 Timothy 4:1-8, identify the illustrations Paul uses to encourage Timothy. Which word-pictures best depict the character qualities which made Paul a man of lasting impact? What is the message Paul conveys in his charge to Timothy?

RESPOND ...

Principle: Changed lives are the currency of heaven. Therefore, success is best measured by lasting fruit, not by immediate results.

1. Return to previous studies where you listed people who have influenced your life. What is the spiritual inheritance you received from them? Have you passed this along to others?

2. How do you want to be remembered? What needs to change in your life for this to become a reality? Name one practical step you can take this week to either begin or continue this process in your life.

3. Spend time in prayer with the members of your group (or as an individual), asking God to make each person a man or woman who leaves a lasting legacy.

CHAPTER 12
LESSONS LEARNED

A young pastor met me at the airport. He shook my hand and embraced me as if I was a long-lost friend. "I've been waiting to meet you," he said as he grabbed my luggage and headed for the exit. "I've heard so much about you and now I finally get to meet you."

Either this guy really loves missionaries and did a detailed background check, or he's got me mixed up with someone else. I wonder what he's heard about me?

I'd never met Kendall Schmitke, but he seemed to know me. I would be spending the weekend at this young pastor's church, speaking on missions.

"You don't know who I am, do you?" he asked as we got into his vehicle.

I rolled my eyes as I tried to dig deep in the memory bank, drawing nothing but a blank. "I, ah…You're the pastor, right?"

Kendall laughed. I didn't recognize him. He was too old to be one of the boys I had counseled at camp, and too young to be someone who studied with me at seminary.

"Mark was my youth pastor," Kendall explained. "He told us about the crazy things you did together. He said you were an important part of his spiritual growth."

This was the first time I had met a disciple of one of my disciples. It was interesting to hear stories of times I had spent with Mark from a third party. Some of the details even seemed vaguely familiar. After spending the weekend at his church I could see a resemblance in the way both Mark and Kendall talked and acted. I could see a bit of myself in my young host. It was as if the spiritual DNA of those who had impacted my life was passed down to me and then to others. It was a unique and special privilege to meet one of my spiritual "grand-disciples."

Paul captured the essence of what I felt during the day I met Kendall with the words of 2 Timothy 2:2:

> And the things you have heard me say in the presence of many witnesses entrust to reliable people who will also be qualified to teach others.

I shook my head in amazement as I realized this was what disciple-making and ministry is all about. It's not about teaching material or planning meetings. It's not a matter of keeping your word and showing up for an appointment. It's not a question of selecting the right methodology. It's not even about going to the right conferences or leadership seminars. It's about reproducing the character of Christ in those whom God brings into your life, in order that they can do the same with others.

A disciple becomes like his mentor. Paul is no exception to this rule. His personal application of the lessons he learned with Barnabas are threaded throughout his writings. His letters show the importance of significant relationships with the goal of influencing others towards Christ-like character and godliness. His focus on team- and gift-based ministry along with leadership development does not go unnoticed. His dependence upon the equipping and guidance of the Holy Spirit marked his life. The time Paul spent walking alongside Barnabas, learning and growing from a man who almost goes unnoticed in the Scriptures, reaped eternal benefits.

Three key areas where the DNA of Barnabas is seen in Paul's ministry are worth noting. First, the principle of spiritual multiplication cited in 2 Timothy 2:2 was exemplified by Barnabas. Secondly, Paul gave a number of unlikely candidates a second chance, a lesson he learned from Barnabas. Third, Paul's emphasis on character development and integrity are reflected in the words Luke chose to describe Barnabas: "a good man , full of the Holy Spirit and faith" (Acts 11:24).

"Paul's Pattern for Mentorship" or "The Barnabas Factor"?

I sat and bit my tongue as the person leading the seminar continued. "As we can clearly see," he stated, "Paul's pattern for discipleship was the multiplication of leaders. He wanted Timothy to follow this model and to invest his life into men who would in turn disciple others."

I couldn't take it any longer and thrust my hand in the air, waving it frantically. "Excuse me!" I interjected. "Where do you think Paul learned these lessons?"

Unprepared for the question, the teacher pored over the biblical text, searching for clues. His answer confirmed my suspicions. "Well, I guess he learned this directly from the Lord." This time I really had to bite my tongue.

I've read a number of books and attended seminars where 2 Timothy 2:2 is taught as Paul's secret to successful and lasting ministry. Seldom is there any acknowledgment that this principle was learned in ministry with Barnabas. Rather, it is almost as if this principle dropped from the sky, a part of some mysterious divine revelation that came to Paul. This could not be further from the truth.

Acts 16:1 is the first recorded action of Paul after departing company with Barnabas. Paul left with Silas on a mission to encourage the believers in Syria and the province of Cilicia with the positive message of the Jerusalem Council's letter. Lystra, the second stopover in their journey, was the home of a young convert named Timothy. He lived there with his Jewish mother and Greek father. Paul heard of Timothy's good reputation and saw a potential leader. This was the basis of an invitation to join Paul's newly formed ministry team on the second missionary journey.[1]

Shortly after visiting Lystra, Luke joined the small troop of missionaries in Troas, a port city on the eastern shores of the Aegean Sea. The shift from writing the accounts of Paul's journey from third person plural (*they* came to the border in Mysia, *they* tried to enter Bithynia), to first person plural (*we* put out to sea, from there *we* traveled to Philippi) is an indication of Luke's direct participation on the ministry team. The only background information we have about Luke tells of his medical profession (Colossians 4:14). We know nothing of his conversion to the Christian faith. He became a dear friend of Paul and companion during many years of ministry together.

The rest of the book of Acts and the greetings of Paul's letters are interspersed with the names of colleagues and disciples who came under his ministry. There are few occasions where he is alone. He gathered and trained leaders as he went, often leaving one or two people to lead a newly established work. Paul was not off doing his own thing.

Why did Paul follow this pattern? What was the reasoning behind Paul's bringing people together to work on teams? Barnabas effectively modeled the principle of no "Lone Rangers" in ministry and service to God. Paul was a good learner.

Another facet related to working together with others is Paul's emphasis on ministry based on spiritual gifts. Paul's exhortation for Timothy was to never neglect his spiritual gift which was imparted to him through a prophetic message (1 Timothy 4:14). Timothy was also encouraged to fan into flame the gift of God in him (2 Timothy 1:6). Paul's teaching on the spiritual gifts in the books of Romans and 1 Corinthians is the most extensive treatment of the subject. Paul was imperative about the importance of the filling of the Holy Spirit (Ephesians 5:18). This was complemented with a focus on the fruit of the Spirit and results of a life lived in the Spirit (Galatians 5:22-24; Ephesians 5:19-6:11, Colossians 3:12-4:6, and 1 Thessalonians 5:16-24).

There was a multiplying effect as Paul invested his life into his companions. New churches were planted and leaders were formed at the same time. This was accomplished because Paul was not reluctant to pass along responsibilities and to allow others to experience hands-on training.

Not all the leaders who were left to lead a church felt they were ready for the task. A good part of the personal letters to Timothy is dedicated to the young pastor's sense of inadequacy. Paul did not rush in to replace his young disciple upon the first signs of distress, but rather encouraged him to remain faithful to his calling and gifting. Despite the circumstances that surrounded him and his own insecurities, Timothy was charged to persevere and finish the race set before him.

Paul could do this because he knew the work of encouraging the faith of new believers was not left to him alone. God's promise to equip others and Christ's commitment to build his church prompted the words of Philippians 1:6:

> ...being confident of this, that he who began a good work
> in you will carry it on to completion until the day of Christ Jesus.

As a result Paul was able to pass along responsibilities to others and to trust God to finish the task of producing lasting fruit in the lives of those he left behind.

There comes a time when a protégé needs to go out on their own and rely upon the indwelling presence of the Spirit to work through them to reach those in their sphere of influence. There is a need for wisdom and spiritual sensitivity to know when this moment has arrived. But this is the purpose of investing our lives into those of our disciples. We do not impart our lives so we can form a cozy club of Christ's followers; we do so to change the world and to make an impact for God's Kingdom.

When a disciple goes out to reach others he or she displays a sign of spiritual maturity which should encourage any discipler. It is the fulfillment of 2 Timothy 2:2—what the disciple has learned begins to be reproduced and has a multiplying effect in the lives of others.

Paul's Focus on Character Development

Paul's focus on spiritual and character development produced "reliable people who will also be qualified to teach others" (2 Timothy 2:2).[2] This lesson, first exemplified to Paul by Barnabas, became one of the traits that marked the influence of the two men.

Paul's admonition to Timothy was to continue the pattern of multiplication of disciples, based on personal example. The opening phrase of 2 Timothy 2:2 is, "And the things you have heard me say in the presence of many witnesses entrust to reliable people…" Paul did not live his life hidden from public view. He depicted Christ-likeness for his observers. Paul knew he needed to first live the truth he taught. This would also be the basis for saying, "Follow my example, as I follow the example of Christ" (1 Corinthians 11:1).

Timothy was encouraged to overcome his sense of youthful inadequacy by being an example for the believers in speech, life, love, faith and purity (1 Timothy 4:12). He was also admonished to watch his life and doctrine closely (1 Timothy 4:16). All that Timothy would do or teach needed to flow out of who he was, not what he did. His character and integrity were the key to having an impact for God.

Some read Paul's exhortations to follow his example, or for Timothy to live a life worthy of being followed, and think: "That's OK for a spiritual giant like Paul or a growing leader like Timothy, but what about me? If mentoring depends upon my personal example I might as well give up right now!"

Be patient. A fallacy which has crept into some teaching on mentorship is that Paul was a masterful communicator and ideal example from the moment of his conversion. But recall the fourteen years he spent before he stepped onto the platform of leadership. Consider the years he spent getting "fine-tuned" with Barnabas. Like Paul, in God's perfect timing, each person can grow into an example of His grace and craftsmanship.

This does not mean that I should sit around until I feel ready or see lights flashing from heaven, convincing me of God's desire for me to make disciples. I need to be open to investing time and energy into those God brings into my life. My desire to walk and grow in obedience to His Word is part of the example I set. It is not a grave mistake if those under my ministry see my weaknesses and the areas where I need to grow.

Part of the secret of Paul's personal example, much like that of his mentor, was based upon the transforming presence of the Holy Spirit.[3] His unswerving proclamation of "Christ in you, the hope of glory" (Colossians 1:27) recognized God's work in his life and the lives of others. The words Paul wrote in Ephesians 5:18 are best translated by the Phillips translation which says, "Keep on being filled by the Holy Spirit," teaching the daily need for His work and power in the lives of people who live to please God.[4] Christ-like character and spiritual maturity cannot be produced in the life of a believer without that person having a keen awareness of God's divine, indwelling presence.

The multiplication principle of 2 Timothy 2:2 is followed by three illustrations Paul used to highlight character qualities worth building into the life of a disciple: the dedication of a soldier; the discipline of an athlete; and the diligence of a hard-working farmer.

A true disciple is like a dedicated soldier who is able to endure hardship and live a life which pleases his or her commanding officer. His or her own daily concerns are overshadowed by the larger picture of where God is leading or what the heavenly commander wants.

This illustration speaks of the obedience and availability of a disciple. This trait does not depend upon the circumstances or the feelings of a believer. It is not a gift that flutters down from heaven on the day of conversion. It is a determined decision to follow Christ's example when He lay aside His rights in obedience to the Father (Philippians 2:5-8).

Paul went on to compare a follower of Christ to an athlete. Both must compete according to the rules of the game. Paul attested to the possibility of being disqualified from the race of Christian life and ministry (1 Corinthians 9:27 and 1 Timothy 1:18-20). For this reason he spoke of the importance of fighting the good fight, finishing the race, and keeping the faith (2 Timothy 4:7).

When an athlete does not compete according to the regulations, there are shameful results. Ask any Canadian over the age of 30 where they were the day Ben Johnson was stripped of his 1988 Olympic gold medal and you will see what I mean. The painful memories of this event recall a dark chapter in Canadian sports history.

Similarly, when a Christian does not live according to biblical standards of conduct, there are equally damaging consequences. Fallen leaders become a source of scorn and are accused of hypocrisy. Inconsistent believers can become the cause for disbelief, leading people to turn away from the love and grace of God.. A life which reflects the nature and character of God has great impact for God in the world.

The final word picture Paul used to encourage Timothy in his personal character development was that of the hard-working farmer. Diligence and perseverance are qualities which enable the worker to see labor come to fruition.

My grandfather came to North America in the mid-1920s. He was attracted to Canada by the offer of freedom and cheap land. As one of the latecomers of the wave of immigration, he purchased a parcel of land in the northern forest regions of the province of Manitoba. The arduous task of clearing the land and preparing it for planting was part of my dad's childhood memories. For many years it seemed the soil produced more rocks than wheat. However, perseverance paid its dividends and a productive farm was eventually carved out of the forest. My grandfather would express a sense of accomplishment and fulfillment as he told the story of his "rock farm."

Patience, perseverance, and diligence are spiritual character qualities that are developed over time. They strengthen us in the hard times, and push us on in our periods of dryness. They are rooted in the faithfulness of God to His people. They are characteristics that come to mind when we read Paul's words in Philippians 3:14: "I press on toward the goal to win the prize for which God has called me heavenward in Christ Jesus."

All three illustrations spoke to Timothy about character development. Timothy was bogged down by a sense of inadequacy as a young minister. This is understandable. Who in their right mind would want to follow the dynamic pastorate of Paul in the church in Ephesus? But in the midst of these circumstances Paul wrote to encourage Timothy and to remind him that what Timothy did or the position he held was not nearly as important as who he was. Character and integrity always come before accomplishments for the Kingdom of God.

Paul: Champion of Those Who Needed a Second Chance

If anyone ever should have understood the need for giving Mark a second chance, it should have been Paul. Although Barnabas had been the one who took a risk on him, presenting him to the leaders in Jerusalem, Paul was unable to extend the same favor to Mark when Barnabas suggested the restoration of their former partner (Acts 15:36-41).

Through the years, however, something changed in Paul's attitude. His demand for a high standard of character never wavered, but he showed a deeper understanding of what it meant to extend God's grace and forgiveness. Later in life Paul would call himself the worst of sinners (1 Timothy 1:15) and zealous persecutor of the church (Galatians 1:13-14). He would be the one to stand up for Timothy and to encourage him in his ministry. Paul would travel with a number of Greeks and defend their cause against legalistic believers who did not want fellowship with non-Jews. Finally, Paul's reevaluation of Mark's personal ministry, asking Timothy to seek and bring to him this useful servant (2 Timothy 4:11), would show his change of mind.

Timothy was included in Paul's missionary troop because the believers of Lystra spoke well of him (Acts 16:2). While Timothy's character is never questioned in the Scriptures, the issues of his youthfulness, fears, and questionable lineage are hurdles Timothy faced. He felt the pressures of temptations, and struggled in knowing how to deal with older believers. When he faced Jewish leaders he knew he would be considered a half-breed as his father was not Jewish. All of these factors weighed against Timothy, but Paul saw beyond them. Paul's focus on godliness and integrity caused him to give unswerving approval to Timothy.

Paul was the Apostle to the Gentiles, and stood firm in supporting them and including them on his ministry teams. The long list of participants on those ministry teams included Luke, Epaphras, Priscilla and Aquila, as well as many others. Paul never feared appearances before Roman leaders, welcoming such conversations as opportunities to share the Gospel. His association with non-Jews brought him criticism and reproach from some, but was a hallmark of his personal ministry. While others were exclusive and didn't care to share the good news with "foreigners," Paul was inclusive and believed that God's grace and forgiveness was for all people.

Paul extended God's forgiveness to all levels of society, even to a death-row candidate named Onesimus. As a rebellious slave who fled his master, he would be beaten severely and ran the risk of death by crucifixion.[5] Paul's plea for leniency and reinstallation went against the cultural practices, even in the homes of Christian masters. Paul, who was the beneficiary of God's grace, implored Onesimus' owner Philemon to go beyond forgiving Onesimus to receiving him as a brother in Christ. This was a radical expression of Paul's willingness to extend a second chance to all people, whether they be rich or poor, influential or common.

Onesimus was fortunate he did not meet Paul earlier. Paul's unbending position and rejection of Mark strikes a contrast with the gentle spirit with which the letter to Philemon is written. Paul had become a champion of undeserving and unlikely candidates for God's grace and forgiveness.

Mark's ministry would be reevaluated and affirmed in Paul's later years. His instruction to Timothy was "Get Mark and bring him with you, because he is helpful to me in my ministry" (2 Timothy 4:11b). It's not known whether the men encountered each other at some time, nor if any formal request for forgiveness ever took place. An older, perhaps mellower Paul now saw Mark as a helpful and seasoned worker.

I wonder if Barnabas ever read those words? If he did he probably shook his head, smiled, and remembered conversations with Paul many years before. Paul had changed and could see the value of giving people the benefit of the doubt and a second opportunity. This was a lesson he learned from his mentor.

Someone once asked me, "When do you give up on a person?" I've struggled with the question, as I have to admit it is an attractive alternative in some cases. In fact, I have given up on some people before my colleagues who insisted on giving someone a third or fourth opportunity.

The F.A.T. acronym—Faithful, Available, and Teachable—has helped me to set standards I communicate at the beginning of a formal mentoring relationship.[6] An informal approach to a mentoring relationship can fall short because of undefined parameters of the relationship. I've suggested a halt to meeting with some who began times of mentorship only to show an apparent lack of interest—sometimes this has resulted in a renewed spark of growth. And I struggle when a person keeps coming back with the same problem, especially if he does not heed or put into practice my advice.

Nonetheless, my "determining factor" or "bottom line" for continuing is that a person comes back for more, wanting to grow and spend time together.

Paul was a good learner. Many of the lessons he learned from Barnabas are mirrored in his actions. Paul's commitment to team ministry and the principle of multiplication was evident, as he took two or three men with him wherever he went. He taught the importance of integrity in the life of leaders. Paul became the champion of those who needed a second chance, a quality that marked the initial stages of his relationship with Barnabas.

Paul would later articulate many of the principles he acquired, applying them to specific situations and the lives of his reading audience. His ability to use the written word, through the inspiration of the Holy Spirit, is part of the rich legacy we share as believers in Jesus Christ. But his impact upon the world causes me to ask the question: What would have become of Saul of Tarsus if it hadn't been for Joseph of Cyprus, also known as Barnabas?

Study Guide

ACTIVE LEARNING ...

Write a sentence that uses each of the following expression to describe either the partnership of Barnabas with Saul, or Paul's relationship with Timothy.

Like father; like son.	*Spitting image.*	*Mirror Image.*
Like two peas in a pod.	*Out of the same mold.*	*Copy-cat*

Share your phrases with the larger group or with another person.

CONSIDER ...

Read the following passages, comparing the references to the life of Paul with those of the life of Timothy. In what ways does Timothy reflect his mentor? Are there any similarities the two men share with Barnabas?

Paul		Timothy
1.	Acts 9:15-22	1 Tim. 4:14 and 2 Tim. 1:6-7
2.	Acts 9:26-30	1 Timothy 4:12
3.	Acts 13:1-3	1 Timothy 2:1-2, 8
4.	Acts 14:1-7	2 Tim. 2:15; 3:15-17
5.	Acts 23:9-11	1 Timothy 1:18-20; 4:1-7
6.	Galatians 5:22-24	1 Timothy 6:11-12
7.	Philippians 4:10-13	1 Timothy 6:3-8

RESPOND ...

Principle: A disciple will become like his or her mentor, reflecting the same character traits and multiplying the impact of a person.

1. Draw your personal "family tree" of spiritual influence. Who were the people who influenced your mentors? Who are the people you have influenced? How many generations of disciples can you trace? How does this exercise enhance your understanding of spiritual multiplication?

2. Identify one way in which you are like the person who mentored you. How much of this do you credit to their influence?

3. Write out the words of 2 Timothy 2:2, replacing Paul's name with your mentor. Add your name, as well as the names of the people you have influenced. Read this prayer aloud, asking God to make you a disciple maker.

EPILOGUE:
A TRIBUTE TO THE TRAINER OF TRAINERS

As I close, I'd like to address the readers of this book who may be a modern-day "Barnabas." Some of you may feel that your ministry is not as significant as that of others who hold important positions or are more vocal. There is good news for you!

The Scriptures give dozens of examples of people like Barnabas. Study the lives of Bible characters and get to know them. Don't go to the All-Star list, but check out some of the unsung heroes. You might be surprised how much of yourself you see in them. I know I did.

What has captured my attention about the life of Barnabas is the way God used an ordinary person to make an extraordinary impact upon the world. I've also grown in my appreciation of who God made me to be, and to let go of a need to focus on His work in the lives of others. These truths give me freedom and a sense of purpose as I seek to serve God. My life can make a difference—and so can yours.

As I've written these pages, an array of faces have come to mind. Some were the men and women God used to shape and mold my life, their influence leaving an unforgettable impression of godliness. I've reminisced about the people who have crossed my path and who look to me as one of their mentors. Another group has loomed in the shadows, their faces not quite in the light of day. They represent those to whom I will minister in the future, including readers of this book. As I've made myself available to God these people keep showing up in my life.

My purpose for writing this book was two-fold. First, I wanted to pay tribute to Barnabas, a person who left a lasting impact for God upon his world. Second, I have sought to encourage those who can identify with what I have shared. Your role and spiritual gifts are an important part of God's work in this world. The Church needs more people like Barnabas and like you.

As you open yourself to God, you might be surprised by the ways He will use you. You might question His wisdom about those He brings into your life. The circumstances He uses to make you a blessing to others might seem odd. But you will have no doubts when He has used you in the life of another person. Whether others have seen you or not doesn't matter. If you are like Barnabas, you will just keep on doing what you do best—impacting people for God.

I close with one last illustration. (If you haven't figured it out by now, I'm more of a storyteller than a preacher. That's part of my gifting and who God made me to be.) I'm also known for always having a full car. I see my vehicle as a tool God gave me to bless others. As far as I'm concerned, "There's always room for one more!"

One day Charles rode with me. He was a student at our leadership training school. In Mexico City terms we were "neighbors" and drove to classes together. Our trip would take anywhere between forty-five minutes to two hours, depending on traffic. We were returning from a class when I asked him some leading questions. I wanted to see if my teaching was getting through. His answer surprised me.

"So, what did you think of the ice-breaker at the beginning of the class?" I asked.

"It was OK."

"How about the small group dynamic we did at the end?"

"That was good too."

"Did you think the overheads were funny?" There was no response.

A little frustrated with his lack of appreciation for my teaching abilities, I finally made a final attempt to provoke his affirmation. "What was the best part of the class?"

His answer brought me back to reality.

"To tell you the truth, the studies are all interesting, but I learn more from our time together driving back and forth than from the time we spend in class."

You could hear the hot air of pride and self-accomplishment rushing out of my proverbial balloon. There was a fairly long pause and I'm sure Charles thought he had said something wrong. That was far from the truth.

I was confronted by a misconception which had crept into my thinking. I had thought that the content of what I was teaching was the primary focus—passing along information and creatively communicating God's truth. But the most important part of my ministry to Charles happened when I wasn't even consciously doing anything. I shared my life with him as we drove and talked. Ministry was done as we helped each other move. A hospital visit when his wife gave birth to their second child is one of my fondest memories of our time together. And I thought I was in Mexico City to teach Bible and mentor young leaders!

The Old Testament equivalent of this principle is found in Deuteronomy 6:6-9. Although intended for the instruction and upbringing of children, this passage speaks of the importance of "teaching as you go."

The impact we make for God can happen in odd places. We teach as we travel together and as we sit down for a meal. More can be taught about hospitality by having someone into your home than in a twelve-week Bible study. There is nothing like traffic gridlock to examine firsthand whether the teacher really knows anything about patience. We model godly living when are confronted with situations which test our integrity. We teach as we walk, as we ride, and as we talk. Our example is being watched at all times, not only when we are up in front of a class.

I trust you have been challenged to make your M.I.F.G—Maximum Impact for God. My desire is for you to realize the important role you play in the Kingdom of God as you share your life with others. My prayer is for your character to reflect Christ-likeness and a life worth emulating. As you impart your life to others I hope you can say, "Follow me as I am also following Christ" (1 Corinthians 11:1).

Hold on for a minute. Are those not the words of the Apostle Paul? Yes, indeed they are. But where did he learn this principle? Could it be…?

Barnabas left no sermon or recorded discourse in the New Testament. There is no confirmation of his methodology or credentials as a teacher.

His only legacy is a life worthy of following.

I pray for an army of men and women who would be like Barnabas, full of the Holy Spirit and faith, able to teach others. It is through these people that God will change our world...one life at a time.

ENDNOTES

Introduction:

[1] J.I. Packer, Merril C. Tenney, and William White Jr., editors, *The Bible Almanac* (Nashville: Thomas Nelson Publishers, 1980) p. 661 and p. 665. The name Saul means "asked," indicating a person who was chosen for a specific task. The name Paul comes from the Latin word, *Paulus*, meaning "little," or "insignificant."

Chapter 1: First Things First

[1] Paul L. Maier, *Eusebius: The Church History*, (Grand Rapids, MI: Kregel Publications, 1999), p. 47 and 58.
[2] See Deuteronomy 10:9 and Joshua 13:14. God's provision for the priestly tribe of Levi was to be accomplished through the faithful giving and sacrifices of the other tribes of Israel.
[3] Eunice Smith, "BF Chpt 01," private email message to Dwayne K. Buhler, 16 December 2002.
[4] Dr. J. Robert Clinton, *The Making of a Leader*, (Colorado Springs, CO: NavPress, 1988), p. 63. I recommend this book as an excellent study of the process and experiences that God uses in the developmental stages of a leader's life.
[5] *Ibid*, p. 74.

Chapter 2: Someone's Knocking at the Door

[1] *Vine Diccionario Expositivo de Palabras del Antiguo y Nuevo Testamento Exhaustivo*, (Nashville, TN: Editorial Caribe Inc., 1999), a Spanish language translation of *Vine's Complete Expository Dictionary of Old and New Testament Words*, (Nashville, TN: Thomas Nelson Inc., 1984) s.v., "*oikos*," p. 146-147.
[2] William Hendricksen, *New Testament Commentary: Galatians and Ephesians*, (Grand Rapids, MI.: Baker Book House, 1968), p. 70-73, and Merril C.

Tenney, *New Testament Survey* (Grand Rapids, MI: Wm. B. Eerdman's Publishing Company, 1961), pages 254 and 274.

[3] The name of this person has been changed to protect his identity.

[4] *Stickability* is a phrase I learned from Gernot Kunzelmann, former director of the Capernwray Bible School in Schladming, Austria. "Mr. K." used this term to speak of perseverance and consistency in the Christian's life. I use this phrase to emphasize the importance of a life that goes the distance and finishes the race God has called us to complete (cf. 2 Timothy 4:7).

Chapter 3: An Invitation to Those Who Can't Swing a Hammer

[1] Paul Ens, *Rutas de Capacitación,* an unpuplished membership manual for the *El Encuentro* church in Mexico City. The actual phrase in Spanish is *"Información sin transformación es una decepción."*

[2] *Evangelical Dictionary of Theology,* Walter A. Elwell, ed., s.v. 'Time' (Grand Rapids, MI: Baker Book House, 1984), pgs. 1094-1096 and *Vine's Complete Dictionary of Old and New Testament Words,* (Spanish version), s.v. *"Tiempo"* (Time), p. 896-898.

Chapter 4: Tiddlywinks is not a Team Sport

[1] The qualities Saul displayed as a disciple of Barnabas will be further discussed in Chapter 5.

[2] Richard J. Higgins, "Process Items," Tape #4 in a Columbia International University Extension Course, Foundations of Ministry (MIN 5900), (Columbia, SC: Columbia International University, 2000).

[3] Chapter 8 deals with the issue of allowing those we disciple to grow and develop, perhaps surpassing our own ministry effectiveness.

Chapter 5: Diary of a Discipler

[1] The introduction to this book describes the Driftwood Principle.

[2] I first heard the F.A.T. acronym used by Dann Spader of Sonlife Youth Ministries. The youth discipleship material that he presented teaches biblical principles that apply to all areas of ministry.

[3] Rick Warren, *Maintaining Your Spiritual Strength* (Ephesians 6:10-11), a recorded message in the Leadership Lifter series of audio tapes.

[4] The list of spiritual gifts in Romans 12:6-8 is often referred to as the ministerial gifts. The seven elements mentioned are prophecy, service, teaching, encouraging, contributing, leadership, and mercy.

Chapter 6: Would Someone Answer the Phone!

[1] *The Call* was written by Dave and Cheryl Fowler. They participated as actors and later as co-directors of the Canadian Bible College ministerial drama team "The Portrait Players."
[2] In Chapter 3, *An Invitation to Those Who Can't Swing a Hammer*, I have addressed the difference between *kairos* and *chronos* time. I define *kairos* time as God's acting in our lives in such a way that He brings significant people at a specific time to meet a specific need. This is all orchestrated in such a way that people, circumstances, and timing all work together for Him to accomplish His purposes in our lives.
[3] See the story in the introduction to Chapter 3: *An Invitation to those who Can't Swing a Hammer.*
[4] Well known author and speaker Ravi Zacharias is the founder and president of *Ravi Zacharias Ministries International*, an Atlanta-based organization.
[5] This phase was discussed in detail in Chapter 5, "Diary of a Discipler."
[6] Dr. Arnold L. Cook, "1978 MIFG Quote," private email message to Dwayne Buhler, 06 February 2003. Dr. Cook coined the phrase 'MIFG' Maximum Impact For God in 1978. He describes the MIFG Principle as "the bottom line of discovering God's will," adding that "the concept is found in the testimony of Paul (Philippians 3:12)." He challenged Christians to make an eternal impact for the Kingdom of God.

Chapter 7: Home Is Where The Suitcase Is

[1] Chapter 8, *They Spelled My Name Wrong*, will deal with the implications of this name change, both for Barnabas and Paul.
[2] Guthrie, Donald, editor, et. al, *The New Bible Commentary Revised*, (Grand Rapids, MI: Wm. B. Eerdman's Publishing Co., 1970), p. 991. An altar near Lystra records the dedication to Zeus, the chief deity in the Greek hierarchy of gods, as the "hearer of prayers."
[3] *Ibid*, p. 991. A statue in Lystra states that Hermes as the chief speaker of the gods, a role that was now identified with Paul.
[4] 1 Peter 1:11 uses the imagery of "living stones" to describe the individuals who make up the Church.

5 "Pero Que Mala Pata!," *La Reforma*, (Mexico City Newspaper), 18 May 2002, Sección Deportes, p. 1.
A direct translation of the title of this article would be "But what a bad foot!" A dynamic translation of the same title would be "Putting your worst foot forward."

Chapter 8: They Spelled My Name Wrong!

1 Billy Graham, *Tal Como Soy*, (Miami, FL: Editorial Vida, 1997), translation by Luis Bernal Lumpuy, p. 41-49. This is a Spanish translation of *Just as I Am*, (New York: Harper Collins Publishers, 1997).
2 J. Wilbur Chapman, *The Life and Work of D.L. Moody* (originally published in a 1900 book), available as an on-line book from http://www.biblebelievers.com/moody/index.html; Internet; accessed 26 October, 2003.
3 Bernard Ruffin, *Fanny Crosby: The Hymn Writer*, Heroes of Faith Series, (Uhrichsville, OH: Barbour Publishing Inc., 1995), p. 29.
4 *The Bible Almanac*, p. 661 and 665.
6 In Chapter 10, *Agree to Disagree*, I will discuss the parting of ways between Barnabas and Paul.
7 D. Guthrie, and J.A. Moyer, eds., *The New Bible Commentary: Revised*, (Grand Rapids, MI.: Wm. B. Eerdman's Publishing Co., 3rd edition, 1970), p. 921.
8 Brian and Norma Bowen work with Campus Crusade for Christ. They have organized several campaigns using the *JESUS* film as an evangelistic tool to reach cities in various countries.

Chapter 9: United We Stand

1 Acts 15:12 reverts to referring to Barnabas and Paul, not to Paul and Barnabas. This is only the second exception to the pattern Luke follows after the events of Acts 13:9, where Saul begins to be called Paul. The protocol of the Council of leaders gives recognition to Barnabas as the leader of the Antiochian envoys. The reference to the two men in the Council's letter followed this pattern (Acts 15:25). However, one of the outcomes of the Jerusalem Council is that Paul left as an authoritative and recognized leader.

Chapter 10: Agree to Disagree

[1] *Evangelism Explosion III*, founded by Dr. James Kennedy, speaks of "divine appointments" which lead to the conversion of people being visited by evangelistic teams.

[2] Galatians 2:11-14 records the visit of Peter to Antioch. During this visit he is accused of hypocrisy, as his behavior towards the Gentile believers changed dramatically when Jewish believers of the "circumcision group" also paid a visit. Paul comments that "even Barnabas was led astray" by Peter's actions (2:13), indicating his disapproval. This event took place after the Jerusalem Council and before the disagreement between Paul and Barnabas, most likely during the period of ministry and teaching recorded in Acts 15:35.

[3] Chapter 7, *Home is Where the Suitcase Is*, deals with the issue of spiritual gift discovery and a sense of being "at home" in ministry.

[4] George Barna, *The Power of Vision: How You Can Capture and Apply God's Vision for Your Ministry*, (Ventura, CA: Regal Books, 1992).

[5] See Chapter 11, *Which Way Did He Go?*

Chapter 11: Which Way Did he Go?

[1] The reference to Barnabas as the 15th Apostle considers the twelve disciples, Matthias—who replaced Judas Iscariot (Acts 1:26)—as the thirteenth, and Paul as the fourteen Apostle.

[2] Kenneth Scott Latourette, *A History of Christianity: Volume 1 – Beginnings to 1500*, (New York: Harper & Row Publishers, 1953 and 1975), p. 288.

[3] The death of Barnabas is usually dated at 61 A.D. at Salamis, the eastern port city of Cyprus.

[4] *The Catholic Encyclopedia: Volume II (Online Edition, 2003)*, s.v. "St. Barnabas"; available from http://www.newadvent.org/cathen/02300a.htm; Internet; accessed 10 Oct. 2003.

[5] Eusebius, *Historia Ecclesiae II*, p. 16.

[6] Earle E. Cairns, *Christianity Through the Centuries*, (Grand Rapids, MI: Academie Books – Zondervan Publishing House, 1951 and 1982), p. 75.

[7] Anglican Church of Canada, "St. Barnabas"; available from http://www.barnabas.ca/anglican-connection.shtml; Internet; accessed 08 Oct. 2003.

[8] William Byron Forbush, ed., *Fox's Book of Martyrs* (Grand Rapids, MI: Zondervan Publishing House, 18th printing, 1980), p. 5.

[9] Wesley Center On-Line, "*The Acts of Barnabas*"; available from http://wesley.nnu/noncanon/acts/actbarn.htm; Internet; accessed 08 Oct. 2003.

[10] Tertullian, *De Pudicitia XX.*

Chapter 12: Lessons Learned

[1] Acts 16:3 mentions Paul's circumcision of Timothy, as he was the child of a Greek father and Jewish mother. This is an apparent inconsistency with the actual message Paul would deliver to the groups of believers in Asia-Minor. Luke reports Paul's justification of this act was appease the Jewish community in Lystra, who knew of Timothy's background.

[2] Eunice Smith, "BF Chpt 12," private email message to Dwayne K. Buhler, 17 October 2003. Eunice Smith is a retired Greek teacher and one of the people who reviewed this project. She reminded me that the word used in 2 Timothy 2:2 could be translated "men and women." The Greek word *anthropos* (ανθρωποσ) was used, allowing for a generic translation (i.e. mankind). The word *aner* (ανηρ), would be translated exclusively "men."

[3] The first biblical references to Barnabas is; "he was a good man, full of Holy Spirit and faith" (Acts 11:24).

[4] Billy Graham, *The Holy Spirit: Activating God's Power In Your Life* by Billy Graham (Waco, TX: Word Books, 1978), p. 121. Dr. Graham explains that the command to be filled with the Spirit is not intended as a once-for-all event, but rather a daily process in the life of the believer.

[5] Walter A. Elwell, *Evangelical Dictionary of Theology*, (Grand Rapids, MI: Baker Book House, 1984), s.v. "slavery," p. 1022.

[6] See Chapter 5, *Diary of a Discipler.*

ABOUT THE AUTHOR

Dwayne Buhler is an author, teacher and pastor. He serves as Lead Pastor of a local church in Kitchener, Ontario, Canada. He is a graduate of Canadian Bible College (Regina, SK) and Regent College (Vancouver, BC). He and his wife, Rhonda, served 15 years as missionaries in Brazil and Mexico before returning to Canada in 2004. Dwayne enjoys a good cup of coffee, a sizzling Brazilian *churrasco* (bar-b-que) and longs walks with Rhonda and their energetic Australian Shepherd, Aspen. Dwayne's focus as he speaks and writes is to teach the Word of God, mentor leaders of the next generation and encourage people of all ages to live out the words of Jesus:

As the Father has sent me, I am sending you.

John 20:212 NIV

For more information see www.dwaynebuhler.com

Made in the USA
Middletown, DE
26 March 2019